LMBD

Developing
Professional
Education

SRHE and Open University Press Imprint
General Editor: Heather Eggins

Titles recently published include:

Michael Allen: *The Goals of Universities*
Sir Christopher Ball and Heather Eggins: *Higher Education into the 1990s*
Ronald Barnett: *The Idea of Higher Education*
Tony Becher: *Academic Tribes and Territories*
Robert Berdahl *et al.*: *Quality and Access in Higher Education*
Hazel Bines and David Watson: *Developing Professional Education*
William Birch: *The Challenge to Higher Education*
David Boud *et al.*: *Teaching in Laboratories*
Heather Eggins: *Restructuring Higher Education*
Colin Evans: *Language People*
Gavin J. Fairbairn and Christopher Winch: *Reading, Writing and Reasoning: A Guide for Students*
Oliver Fulton: *Access and Institutional Change*
Derek Gardiner: *The Anatomy of Supervision*
Gunnar Handal and Per Lauvås: *Promoting Reflective Teaching*
Vivien Hodgson *et al.*: *Beyond Distance Teaching, Towards Open Learning*
Jill Johnes and Jim Taylor: *Performance Indicators in Higher Education*
Margaret Kinnell: *The Learning Experiences of Overseas Students*
Peter Linklater: *Education and the World of Work*
Graeme Moodie: *Standards and Criteria in Higher Education*
John Pratt and Suzanne Silverman: *Responding to Constraint*
Kjell Raaheim *et al.*: *Helping Students to Learn*
John Radford and David Rose: *A Liberal Science*
Marjorie Reeves: *The Crisis in Higher Education*
John T.E. Richardson *et al.*: *Student Learning*
Derek Robbins: *The Rise of Independent Study*
Tom Schuller: *The Future of Higher Education*
Geoffrey Squires: *First Degree*
Ted Tapper and Brian Salter: *Oxford, Cambridge and the Changing Idea of the University*
Gordon Taylor *et al.*: *Literacy by Degrees*
Kim Thomas: *Gender and Subject in Higher Education*
Malcolm Tight: *Higher Education: A Part-time Perspective*
Malcolm Tight: *Academic Freedom and Responsibility*
Susan Warner Weil and Ian McGill: *Making Sense of Experiential Learning*
David Watson: *Managing the Modular Course*
Thomas G. Whiston and Roger L. Geiger: *Research and Higher Education*
Gareth Williams: *Changing Patterns of Finance in Higher Education*
Alan Woodley *et al.*: *Choosing to Learn*
Peter W.G. Wright: *Industry and Higher Education*
John Wyatt: *Commitment to Higher Education*

Developing Professional Education

Hazel Bines and David Watson

The Society for Research into Higher Education
& Open University Press

Published by SRHE and
Open University Press
Celtic Court
22 Ballmoor
Buckingham
MK18 1XW

and

1900 Frost Road, Suite 101
Bristol, PA 19007, USA

First Published 1992

*A catalogue record of this book is available from
the British Library*

Library of Congress Cataloging-in-Publication Data

Bines, Hazel.
    Developing professional education:a polytechnic perspective/by
Hazel Bines and David Watson; with John Astley . . . [et al.].
        p.   cm.
    Includes bibliographical references and index.
    ISBN 0-335-09711-1. – ISBN 0-335-09710-3 (pbk.)
    1. Professional education–England–Oxford–Case studies.
2. Curriculum planning–England–Oxford–Case studies.   3. Oxford
Polytechnic.   I. Watson, David, 1949– .   II. Title.
LC1059.B55   1992   91-33758
378'.013'0942574–dc20   CIP

Typeset by Graphicraft Typesetters Ltd, Hong Kong
Printed in Great Britain by St Edmundsbury Press Ltd
Bury St Edmunds, Suffolk

Contents

Foreword

As we approach the end of the twentieth century, higher education and the world of work are increasingly being urged to work together to meet social and economic priorities. Training, directed towards the acquisition of skills and competences, and education, directed towards acquisition of knowledge and development of self-critical reflection, are also on a converging and mutually reinforcing path.

In some senses not much of this is new. International comparisons with our national record of participation in post-compulsory education, as well as of the outcomes in terms of highly-skilled personnel, have been debated between government, educational providers and employers at least since the Royal Commissions of the late nineteenth century. When we get behind the data war of the government and educational statisticians, it remains true that education, industry, and the professions *must* work together to fill skills gaps and to supply people of vision and judgement in order to meet our immediate and long-term objectives.

In *Developing Professional Education*, Hazel Bines, David Watson, and their colleagues, demonstrate the ways in which these challenges impact upon an individual, but not untypical, institution of higher education. Their unpicking of the generic issues, supported by the case studies which the individual chapters introduce, emphasizes the need for professional education to receive appropriate esteem, planning priority, and developmental attention within our polytechnics, colleges and universities. Together they present a positive, forward-looking and encouraging story. I am sure that it will prove of value to all parties involved in the vital task of developing professional education.

Sir Bryan Nicholson
Chairman and Chief Executive
The Post Office
Chairman
National Council for Vocational Qualifications

Notes on Contributors

John Astley has lectured in sociology in the Department of Social Studies. He is a sociologist of culture, his main research interest over many years being the interrelation between youth and popular cultures. His involvement in designing and delivering curricula in sociology and social policy for professional practitioners has also led to a particular interest in 'professional cultures' and the management of change, together with ways in which 'people-workers' learn their roles. He has now returned to a lecturing post at Oxford College of Further Education.

Hazel Bines studied sociology before training as a primary teacher, following which she worked for 13 years in primary, secondary and special schools in South Yorkshire. She then undertook her doctoral research on policy and provision for special educational needs in secondary schools, at the University of Oxford. She was appointed as a Senior Lecturer in Education at Oxford Polytechnic in 1986 and is currently one of the Deputy Heads of the School of Education, with particular responsibility for academic development, including both initial and CPD courses. She has written and contributed to both books and journal articles on special educational needs, and as well as maintaining her particular interest in teacher education, has been involved in the general development of professional education at Oxford Polytechnic.

Stuart Brown is Information Systems Manager. He is responsible, within the Computer Services Department, for the business and office automation systems used in the management and administration of the institution. Stuart is currently establishing and exploiting software engineering methods and technology for the particular purposes of the Polytechnic.

Ruth Champion is Head of the Department of Health Care Studies, a department which was created to accommodate the pre-registration degrees in nursing and midwifery for Oxfordshire Health Authority. She has been involved in developing degrees for health care professionals for 15 years and is committed to practice-based professional education.

Anne Dufton is Deputy Director, Corporate Planning and Marketing. Her research interests in interprofessional approaches to training stem from close association with the development of courses for teachers, social workers, nurses and midwives, health visitors and district nurses and a range of professions allied to medicine including occupational therapy, physiotherapy and speech therapy. With Harry Webster, she pioneered the first inter-professional degree course for teachers and social workers in the (then) Ulster Polytechnic. She is currently a member of UKCC Council and its Educational Policy and Health Visitor Committees and of the Occupational Therapy Board of the CPSM.

Diane Gaunt is the principal lecturer responsible for award-bearing inservice education for teachers provided by the School of Education, and has been instrumental in developing a new INSET scheme. She has taught in higher education in Britain, New Zealand and South Africa as well as in further education colleges and schools. Her research interests focus on vocational education with special emphasis on the professions.

Peter George is Review Group Chair of the Faculty of Life Sciences and has been a teacher of sociology and social policy in the sociology field and in a wide range of professional courses for more than 20 years. His main academic interests are in comparative social policy, welfare ideology and citizenship, but he also has a long-standing interest in the theory and practice of education for the health and social care professions. He was Co-Director of the team which designed the Polytechnic's Nursing and Midwifery degrees in collaboration with the Oxford Schools of Nursing and Midwifery and the Oxfordshire District Health Authority's Nursing and Midwifery Service. More recently he played a key role in the Polytechnic's collaboration with Dorset House School of Occupational Therapy to develop an honours degree in Occupational Therapy.

Clare Gillies is principal lecturer in social work in the Department of Social Studies. She trained to be a probation officer after studying social sciences at Liverpool University. She worked in rural and urban areas as a basic grade and senior probation officer. In 1970 she returned to Liverpool to inaugurate social work education in the Department of Extension Studies at the University. She has been involved in social work education since taking up her post in Oxford Polytechnic in 1976. Her present research compares the quality of service for clients between professional social work and self-help groups, with particular reference to minority groups.

John Glasson is Head of School of Planning. He trained as an economist and planner, and worked in planning practice before joining Oxford Polytechnic. His interests extend over a wide range of environmental issues, and focus in particular on regional planning and development, and socio-economic impact assessment and management. He is Research Director of the Impacts Assessment Unit, and Chair of the Centre for Tourism and Leisure Studies at Oxford. He chaired the CNAA Built Environment Steering Group for the study of interdisciplinarity in the built environment.

Georgina Glenny is a senior lecturer in education in the School of Education. Currently she is Teaching Studies Co-ordinator for the PGCE (Primary) course. She was formerly Course Leader for the Diploma in Professional Studies in Education (Special Educational Needs). Previously she was Head of Special Educational Needs at a comprehensive school in Oxfordshire and also trained as an educational psychologist.

Peter Harris is principal lecturer in Accounting and Course Director of the Master's Degree Programme in the Department of Hotel and Catering Management. He trained in the industry and has held managerial positions in hotels, restaurants and banqueting operations. In addition to the HCIMA professional qualification he holds the Certified Diploma in Accounting and Finance and a Master's degree by research from the University of Strathclyde. In 1990 he was elected Honorary Fellow of the British Association of Hotel Accountants for his contribution to hospitality accounting education. Peter Harris is also joint author of two leading textbooks on accounting in the hospitality industry and a visiting professor in managerial accounting on the Cornell University-ESSEC hotel programme in Paris.

Richard Hayward is Deputy Head of the School of Architecture and Co-chair of the Joint Centre for Urban Design. He trained as an architect at Liverpool University where he later completed a programme of research in housing history. He has practised as an architect and urban designer in the public and private sectors in Europe and the USA. His most recent publication is *Architecture: An Invitation* (1990), written with Paul Oliver for Basil Blackwell.

Elizabeth Hickling is a senior lecturer in education in the School of Education. She currently organizes school experience within the BEd (Primary) course and is also Leader of the Early Years specialist track for the MA in Education. She has recently become Course Leader of the re-designed BEd (Primary) course implemented in September 1991. She was formerly Head of a First School in Buckinghamshire.

Steve Hughes was course manager for MBA programmes at the School of Business and senior lecturer in employee relations and organizational behaviour. He spent a number of years in the printing industry before entering full-time education and has been responsible for the design and delivery of a wide range of company-specific training programmes. He is currently researching the industrial relations of autonomous work design in the UK and the development of pluralist industrial relations in Hungary. He is now lecturing in the Department of Management and Labour Relations at the University of Auckland, New Zealand.

Glen McDougall is Deputy Head of the School of Planning with particular responsibility for academic development. A sociologist with considerable experience in planning education, she has been responsible for developing housing education in the School of Planning in recent years. She currently specializes in the teaching of urban social processes, planning theory and social policy and has published in these areas. Current research interests include gender questions in social and planning policies and recent developments in planning theory and practices.

Denise Morrey is Deputy Head of the School of Engineering and Head of Mechanical and Manufacturing Engineering. Her first degree is from Cambridge University and she has had industrial experience with British Rail and Bifurcated Engineering. Her research interests are noise and vibration in vehicles and robotics. She has been based at the Polytechnic since 1984. In this time she has had a wide range of course development and management experience and responsibilities.

Kathy Murphy lectures in the Department of Health Care Studies. She both leads professional modules and is senior tutor for the Nursing and Midwifery degree. Previously she worked in the National Health Service in various roles, from sister in Accident & Emergency to nurse teaching in a school of nursing. She moved to Oxford in 1987 and has since been involved in developments in nurse education there. Her initial degree was in history and anthropology and her higher degree in nursing. Her research interests include cultural issues in nursing, nurse experiences of coming from ethnic minorities, the therapeutic aspects of nursing and the development of professional competence.

Paul Reading is senior lecturer in social work in the Department of Social Studies. After working in the probation service for 10 years, he moved into higher education in 1975. Teaching and research interests centre on mental health issues and he is professional adviser to Oxford MIND. He has written about social work education, probation practice, family reactions to mental illness and the role of voluntary organizations in community care. He was formerly on the editorial board of *Social Work Today*.

Clive Robertson is currently Review Group Chair of the Faculty of Business, Languages and Hotel Management. He has advised a number of companies and organizations on accreditation of their own training programmes and his primary interest is employment-based learning, including assessment of such learning. He has managed two Training Agency funded projects on employment-based learning contracts and a third project on learning contracts in   supervised work experience. He was a founder member and Chair of the Industrial Tutors Group of the Standing Conference on Hospitality Management Education. He is Chair of the Polytechnic's Credit Accumulation and Transfer Committee.

Trevor Watkins is Deputy Director (Quality) at the Polytechnic of the South Bank, London. He was formerly ASDA Professor and Head of the School of Business at Oxford Polytechnic and an Associate Member of the Nottingham Institute of Financial Studies at the University of Nottingham. He has published a number of articles on the marketing of financial services in both trade and academic journals. He is editor of the *International Journal of Bank Marketing* and is senior examiner for the new marketing financial services diploma for the Chartered Institute of Marketing.

David Watson is Director of Brighton Polytechnic. He was previously principal lecturer in humanities at Crewe & Alsager College of Higher Education before becoming Dean of the Modular Course, and then Deputy Director, at Oxford Polytechnic. His academic interests are in the history of American ideas and higher education policy, and his publications include *Margaret Fuller: An American Romantic* (Berg, 1988), and *Managing the Modular Course* (SRHE/Open University Press, 1989), as well as numerous reviews and articles. He is a member of the Councils of CNAA and PCFC.

Introduction and Acknowledgements

This book was conceived as a result of wide-ranging discussion about the development of education for the professions at Oxford Polytechnic. It originally sought to offer distinctive perspectives from a polytechnic on a range of issues involved in course development and delivery, including the growing importance of institutional planning and management, interprofessional cooperation and collaboration between employers, professional bodies and higher education. However, its relevance to all sectors of higher education was an equally strong theme, which has been reinforced by the recommendations of the Government White Paper on further and higher education published in May 1991. *Higher Education: A New Framework* (Cm. 1541) proposes the abolition of funding and other binary divisions across higher education as a whole, while reasserting the importance of the professional and vocational mission of the Polytechnics and Colleges sector. *Education and Training for the 21st Century* (Cm. 1536, 2 vols) proposes sweeping changes in the organization of further education with a view to increasing the opportunities for students with other than traditional sixth form qualifications to move smoothly into higher education. Both underline the themes established here of employer–education partnerships and more flexible patterns of teaching and learning.

This is intended to be a practical book. Both the original concept and its achievement over a period of 18 months are the responsibility of several hands. The main authors are grateful not only to the author of the foreword and the contributors of the case studies but also to many other members of teaching and support staff at Oxford Polytechnic. Special thanks are due to the participants in Polytechnic-wide seminars on post-experience and professional courses (rapidly termed PEP) in June 1989, February 1990 and July 1990.

However, without one person at the hub of all of the activity involved in creating the book it either would not have happened or would have taken an unacceptably long time. Cheryl Codling brought to the task of chasing, word-processing and improving the presentation of this text all of the qualities which have made her indispensable to the Academic Affairs Office within the Polytechnic's Central Management Team. As with *Managing the Modular Course*, from the same publisher, the authors are deeply grateful to her for her efficiency, good humour and general good sense. Latterly, after the free transfer of one of us to another polytechnic, Maureen Barnard also helped to keep the project on track.

Finally, we would like to thank our families for their characteristic forbearance and encouragement. Steve Bines, Betty Skolnick, and Sarah and Michael Watson all assisted us in their own ways.

Hazel Bines
David Watson

1

The Changing Shape of Professional Education

David Watson

Higher education, unlike its apparently less glamorous sister further education, has always had difficulty in defining what it is and what it is trying to
do. A good recent example of sensitivity to this issue is the excellent survey
by Ronald Barnett, *The Idea of Higher Education* (Barnett, 1990). In response
to a variety of pressures, many of them political, terms such as 'relevant'
and 'vocational' have become conspicuous by their overuse. Now they are
in danger of being followed by the term 'professional'.

This book is about 'professional' higher education in the context of a
large, multi-faceted institution. It takes a generous view of the definition
of the term, to include not only the process of education in qualifying to
become a professional, but also the post-experience courses and further study
that justify an individual in *remaining* a professional. The approach is
philosophical only in part; the key aim of the authors is to demonstrate
some of the real-world challenges involved in identifying and satisfying
the many interests involved in the formation and retention of professionals.
But if there is an underlying commitment of the institution described here,
and of the authors collectively, it is to the integration of mainstream and
professional higher education. The advantages of professional education
breaking out of the tight enclave assumed by many of the professional
bodies to be vital to their standards (as well as to less worthy considerations
such as labour supply planning) are manifold: in the cross-fertilization of
student experience; in providing opportunities for deferred choice and
change; as well as for the development of the 'academic' disciplines contributing to professional practice.

In what follows each chapter begins with an overview of contextual and
philosophical issues raised by an aspect of provision of professional courses.
This is then followed by a series of short case studies, all contributed by
practitioners, showing the principles established in action. This introduc-
tory chapter concludes with a comment on the relevant provision at Oxford
Polytechnic, from which the cases are drawn.

The culture of professionalism

What is a 'profession' and how does one become a 'professional'? This question has inspired a lively historiography as well as providing a fertile source for social scientists. Most investigators agree that professionalism is associated with a characteristically modern mode of production, division of labour, and set of cultural relations; that the emergence of a professional cadre or class is of major economic and social significance; and that the internal discipline of professions has a formative influence over patterns of education and intellectual enquiry. Scholars may disagree about the point from which to date the emergence of this phenomenon – suggestions begin with the role of the medieval university – but most interpretations converge upon the late nineteenth century as the critical stage. Subsequent development of the professions in the twentieth century has been seen by some writers as *the* most salient feature of modern society, as illustrated by the classic statement of the structural functionalist sociologist, Talcott Parsons (1968, p. 545):

> It is my view that the professional complex, though obviously still incomplete in its development, has already become the most important single component in the structure of modern societies. It has displaced first the 'state', in the relatively early modern sense of that term, and, more recently the 'capitalistic' organisation of the economy. The massive emergence of the professional complex, not the special status of capitalistic or socialistic modes of organisation, is the crucial structural development in twentieth century society.

In addition to the highly questionable view that professions have replaced both state and capitalism as the driving forces of modern society, such analysis of course rests upon a series of assumptions about the definition of a profession. Sociologists in particular have spent much time and effort in establishing the so-called 'traits' or characteristics of professional activity. The check-list compiled by Waddington in the *Social Science Encyclopedia* includes the following (Waddington, 1985, pp. 650–651):

1. possession of a skill based on theoretical knowledge;
2. provision of training and education;
3. testing of competence of members;
4. organisation;
5. adherence to a code of conduct; and
6. altruistic service.

Waddington also points to more recent dissatisfaction with the circularity and lack of critical sensitivity of this kind of analysis. In particular, it uncritically accepts the professional's self-definition and ignores the ways in which professional rhetoric (for example in claims about community service and altruism) serves to legitimate professional privilege (Johnson, 1972, p. 25). Similarly, 'trait' theory not only assumes the validity of an 'ideal type' which has actually been constructed in a particular (Anglo-American) cultural and historical context, but also ignores some of the most important aspects of the interaction between professions and society. A better question is about the processes through which particular professions seek and obtain (or fail to obtain) professional status, revealing the sources of power available to certain occupational groups (Freidson, 1983; Johnson, ibid.).

Analysis is thus now moving from an implicit acceptance of the special pleading inherent in previous conceptions of professions towards the location of the study of the professions in a wider and historical analysis of occupations in general. Modern scholars have stressed the role of professional *power* both as a goal and as an effect of the organization of the professions. The drive for autonomy in particular (via monopoly and self-regulation) can be shown to cut across ideals of altruism and social service. As a consequence, more comfortable assumptions about the value of professions are increasingly replaced with critiques of their monopolies of knowledge and services, their relationship with clients and the state, and the objective value (or otherwise) to society of professional services. Other relevant trends include the movement from private practice towards salaried employment in large organizations, and the impact of social, political, economic and technological change on the nature of professional knowledge, activities and autonomy.

It is also important not to ignore the *heterogeneity* of the professions in terms of the number of occupations claiming professional status and the range of their autonomy, credibility and practices (Johnson, 1984). This heterogeneity is further increased by differences in national culture and by specialization and segmentation within each particular profession (Bucher and Strauss, 1961; Johnson, ibid.; Waddington, op. cit.).

Nevertheless, from the point of view of providers of education and training to intending and continuing professionals, certain characteristics and effects of professions and professional organization are of particular importance. First, there is the question of *guaranteed competence*; the student's qualifications must mean something in terms of his or her ability to perform certain tasks to a requisite standard. Connected with this is the notice of *licence*; a body, whether the providing institution, or the collectivity of the profession, or both, must take responsibility for accrediting this competence. This, in turn, raises questions about the *independence* or self-regulating role of the profession itself; who, ultimately is responsible for the standards and, for example, for any indemnification owed to society at large in respect of the licence? Finally, all of these issues operate in a context of *expectations*: of society about the skills of the professional, of the professional himself or herself about status and other rewards.

Professional and educational concerns

In working through these issues the potential for disagreement between educators and trainers on the one hand and the professionals, individually and corporately, on the other, is ever-present. The professions, for example, can easily hold views of the following which diverge from those of educationalists.

1. *Entry requirements*. Either party might have more or less flexible approaches to the necessary pre-course experience and qualifications of students. In general the development of more generous approaches to entry requirement by colleges, recognizing non-standard qualification and prior experiential learning, as well as an emphasis on the 'value added' by the educational process, have not been fully matched by professional bodies. The latter frequently express concern about the possible impact on exit standards (see below).
2. *Cohort progression/identity*. Following the notion of professional socialization, professional bodies again tend to be more conservative about the impact of varied pace or mode of study, the possibility of late or deferred choice of routes of study leading to professional qualifications, and the impact of intending professionals and those studying for more general educational measures working together.
3. *Inculcating the culture*. Claims about the general educational aims of courses invariably tend to be larger (and vaguer) than those of professional training (although this may be changing as a consequence of new models of professional practice and responsibility). Conversely, the professions may complain if the courses taken by their new members have not taken the time or trouble to inculcate aspects of working practice or assumptions (or may indeed have gone out of their way to be critical of these).
4. *Exit standards*. In the extreme, this may lead to conflicting views about what the initially qualified professional values, knows, and/or is able to perform. To take a crude example, the educationalist may have greater faith in the transferability from one task to another of the skills he or she has taught than the professional body obliged to licence and indemnify.
5. *Labour supply*. Another motive for professional bodies to control the exit from courses of qualified personnel is their interest variously in increasing or restricting the supply. Protectionism of this kind is much harder to sustain in educational institutions where courses are in general open to all who can achieve the requisite support (fees and maintenance) and who can benefit, intellectually or personally.

Adjudication of all of these potentially contentious issues requires, ideally, a constructive and open-ended dialogue between educational institutions and professional bodies. In the course of this dialogue each partner may influence the other in related ways. At its best the dialogue contributes constructively to development of progressive *models of professional practice* (discussed in Chapter 2). In particular, the appropriate analysis of educational and professional values can assist in the development of a genuinely 'reflective' and self-aware practitioner, whose capacity for originality and creativity is enhanced while maintaining the requisite array of functional competences.

Sponsors, providers and clients

The map of interested parties is, however, broader and more complex than this essential relationship between colleges and professional bodies. Wider issues include the contentious one of who pays for the supply of qualified professionals and how students are attracted onto either initial qualifying courses or programmes of continuing professional development. The underlying set of relationships is at least triangular.

In the first place there are the *sponsors* of professional education and training, ranging from the government in its general support for further and higher education, through employers and professions seeking the supply of suitably qualified entrants and a legitimate return on their tax payments, to the direct sponsorship of individual students. It is in this arena that concerns about the ability of the educational system as a whole to meet society's needs for highly qualified people are most frequently expressed, and a political dialogue develops about who is financially and educationally responsible.

Managing marketing and the supply of courses in this context poses special problems for *providers*, discussed in detail in Chapter 4. Institutions of higher education, in particular, need to balance professional requirements against a spectrum of obligations also including the provision of general higher education (the purposes of which may focus on personal enrichment rather than vocational preparation), research and consultancy, as well as other types of income generation. At least since the implementation in the UK of the Education Act 1988, and the resulting development of relationships with the two main Funding Councils (the Universities Funding Council (UFC) and the Polytechnics and Colleges Funding Council (PCFC)), institutions have been compelled to be more specific about their overall aims and objectives. All PCFC institutions and most universities now plan to meet *mission statements* which invariably refer to vocational and professional education in the contexts of local, regional, national and international needs (PCFC, 1990, p. 118). Oxford Polytechnic's statement reads as follows (emphasis added):

1. To serve society and its economic interests by providing cost-effective higher education of undisputed quality which:

   (a) promotes the personal and intellectual development of every individual;
   (b) is a *relevant preparation for employment*;
   (c) answers to the country's needs for *qualified people in science, technology, business and the professions*;
   (d) makes available opportunities to study at a broad range of levels, of course lengths and of modes (part-time, full-time or mixed);
   (e) offers the possibility of combining different areas of study in ways not generally available elsewhere in the UK;
   (f) has strong links with the local community.

2. To extend higher education opportunities for those who are at present under-represented in higher education; women, mature students, ethnic minorities and the disabled.
3. To facilitate the *continuing personal and professional development of those in work or seeking to re-enter or change work.*
4. *Through applied research and consultancy activities* and courses, *to assist* business, industry, cultural organisations, public services, *the professions*, and the community at large.
5. To contribute to better international understanding by establishing links with institutions abroad, fostering exchanges and admitting students from overseas.
6. To enable all polytechnic staff to develop their potential in fulfilling the aims above.

It should also be noted that providers are increasingly conscious of their own professional practice, especially in respect of new approaches to teaching and learning. Hence the equally frequent reference to staffing needs and staff development in these statements.

The final side of the triangle is that belonging to the students themselves, the *clients*. Like all students in the system, those aiming for professional qualifications, or participating in updating or continuing professional development (CPD) courses, are individuals with personal expectations and life-plans. As such their interests may not always neatly coincide with the intentions for them of either sponsors (who may take a more narrowly instrumental approach to their needs) or providers (who may not always supply the courses they want to take, at a time or in a manner with which they are comfortable). The latter points are picked up particularly in Chapters 2 and 3.

Intending, and especially practising professionals, also tend to be acutely aware of their problems and prospects in the employment market. This is not just a case of economic or social reward (although it perhaps marks another enduring trait of professionals, including those in higher education, that they have rarely been happy with their social status or rates of pay), but raises questions about career flexibility, interprofessional demarcation and intellectual and emotional satisfaction. Many of these issues are discussed in later chapters.

This nexus of sponsors, providers and clients is also located in a context of rapid change in both higher education and the professions, requiring major innovations in professional education which are simultaneously constrained by traditional assumptions and pressures on resources. Uncertainty and change within the professions themselves, resulting from changing work patterns, public and political criticism of their effectiveness and role, and social, economic and technological developments, are currently stimulating considerable demand for new and revised courses and qualifications. Coupled with developments in the pattern and provision of higher education (such as open learning and new systems of credit accumulation and transfer) these demands require major investment in the design and delivery of new courses, new modes of learning and new partnerships with the professional community. However, in the present resource climate, it is often difficult enough to maintain the quality of current provision, let alone ensure its continued development. (This problem is exacerbated by the high demand for human and material resources made by aspects of many professional courses, such as the clinical/practical placement.) In addition, professional education has until recently, often had a low or marginal status within higher education, even in polytechnics, despite their more vocational mission. The 'higher education' culture has traditionally celebrated the primacy of 'pure' rather than 'applied' science, specialist rather than interdisciplinary work, and research rather than teaching (Becher, 1989). Earlier changes in professional education largely took place as a consequence of professional expansion, threats to the material base of the profession, or demands for services from previously disenfranchised groups (Atkinson, 1983). Now its political economy is increasingly determined by a mix of rapid social change, state and other intervention, unpredictable market forces and restricted material and cultural investment.

In summary, institutions of higher education are thus presented with a complex pattern of pressures of demand, supply and quality in designing, delivering and managing professional education. We intend to show, from a polytechnic perspective, many of these challenges and opportunities working out in practice.

The institutional profile

The issues outlined above, together with other aspects of course design, course delivery and course and institutional management, will be addressed in more detail in following chapters. A strong theme developed there is the necessity for a planned institutional framework including an overarching strategy for professional education. Support is also essential from employers and the services themselves. The development of strategic planning and support will necessarily vary from institution to institution. The process is regularly likely to include an audit of current provision, followed by a subsequent evaluation of the profile, the setting of future goals, and establishing the means to realize them. For polytechnics in particular, the need for strategic planning is well established and sharpened by the requirement to develop institutional plans to support the funding and bidding processes now in place through PCFC. Universities are likely to feel the same pressures in coming years.

The audit can have a number of useful functions within the planning process. As well as providing basic information on the range of courses, qualifications and students involved, it will also indicate convergences and divergences across the range of professional education. For most institutions, reflecting the generally slow response to demands for continuing professional development (see Chapter 2), it is likely that the audit will reveal a paucity of CPD courses (particularly at Masters level) no matter what the qualitative or quantitative strength of the pre-service provision.

Interdisciplinary or interprofessional courses have also been slow to develop (see Chapter 5). Balance between different professional areas is more likely to vary from institution to institution, though it will reflect certain patterns. The universities dominate the education of the 'ivy league' professions such as medicine and law, while polytechnics and colleges, until recently at least, have more courses for the 'technical' professions (such as engineering), the newer professions (such as business management) and the 'caring' and often somewhat lower status, professions (such as nursing, social work and teaching). The profile may also well be affected by past amalgamations (particularly the incorporation of teacher training colleges), research funding (supporting, for example, particular forms of engineering) and the profiles of the local economy and neighbouring institutions. Such an audit can reveal unnecessary and overlooked weaknesses in the profile easily remedied by an active approach to course development, local collaboration and effective marketing.

Evaluation and the setting of future targets will in part depend on the goals and resources of the institution as a whole. Nevertheless, certain objectives may be universally desirable, such as a healthy balance between the 'caring' and 'technical' professions, the importance of more interdisciplinary work and the need to develop CPD courses (to respond to both professional demand and demographic changes in the student population). The mapping of possible developments and resources should also draw on more 'hidden' aspects of an institution's activity, such as short courses and consultancy, the degree of information-sharing and collaboration between staff in different areas of professional education, prospects for multi- or inter-professional work with one or more services or employers, and the standing of professional education within the institution as a whole. Lying behind all of these parts is the ethos of the institution as a whole. How much is professional education valued?

The Oxford Polytechnic profile

The profile of professional courses at Oxford Polytechnic (see Appendix, p. 161) illustrates a number of these points, as well as providing a possible model for audit and the context for the case studies in this book. As a medium-sized polytechnic, with a strong general profile and a good reputation for popularity in the recruitment market and the employability of its graduates, it could be expected to have a balanced range of professional courses at pre-service and CPD levels. This is indeed the case, although, reflecting earlier comments, apart from Planning and Teacher Education the number of CPD courses has only recently begun to expand and there are still several professional areas where award-bearing CPD courses need to be developed. The profile also indicates that for various historic reasons, many outside the control of the institution, areas which might have been expected to be well established, such as health care courses, have only recently been initiated. However, a strong relationship with the health authority, and a well-thought-out model of nursing education, coupled with other initiatives in the education of health professionals, have now made health care studies one of the leading areas of professional education in the institution. The particular strengths in the profile, well recognized externally in terms of quality, include planning, hotel and catering management, and the burgeoning field of management education where there are special strengths in distance learning. Teacher education courses are also well established, including a strong profile of CPD consultancy and short course work. Last, but not least, Oxford Polytechnic has the largest School of Architecture in the country.

What is less clear from the formal profile but well illustrated in this book, is the increasingly high degree of consensus over what constitutes 'good practice' in professional education. Nearly all the professional courses focus primarily on developing professional competence and operational practice, while retaining a strong vision of 'reflective' practice. Course design, delivery and management, particularly in clinical/practical placements, reflect an ethos of partnership with the relevant professional community which continues to be developed despite resource and other constraints. The bare profile also does not entirely reflect the growing importance of multi- and inter-disciplinary/professional work. The earlier establishment of interdisciplinary courses in the area of Urban Design has been added to in the area of the Built Environment (see Chapter 5) and a course on Housing Education. Education is also currently contributing to the development of a teaching qualification in the new Health Care Studies degree for qualified health care professionals and a short course on interprofessional work has been developed by Education and Social Work. In addition, the formation of an Interprofessional Group and a number of short conferences and seminars have facilitated the sharing of common problems and concerns, subsequently translated into policy and course development through colleagues from different professional areas serving as members of course planning committees and validation and review panels for professional courses. Various sub-committees of Academic Standards Committee have carried out the audit in this book and made a number of recommendations on policy and practice for professional education, as well as developing schemes to facilitate credit accumulation and transfer (CATS) and the accreditation of employment-based learning. Finally, the Modular Course, in providing a unit-credit based and flexible framework for most undergraduate education in the polytechnic (Watson, 1989), has provided a unique opportunity to integrate professional education with other higher education, as well as a model for ways to develop continuing education. The overall picture is one of 'work in progress', which we trust will be of interest to colleagues in other institutions further or less far down the various pathways which we have mapped.

References

Atkinson, P. (1983) 'The reproduction of the professional community'. In Dingwall, R. and Lewis, P. (eds) *The Sociology of the Professions*. London: Macmillan.
Barnett, R. (1990) *The Idea of Higher Education*. Milton Keynes: SRHE/Open University Press.
Becher, T. (1989) *Academic Tribes and Territories*. Milton Keynes: SRHE/Open University Press.
Bucher, R. and Strauss, A. (1961) 'Professions in process'. *American Journal of Sociology*, **66**, 325–34.
Freidson, E. (1983) 'The theory of professions: state of the art'. In Dingwall, R. and Lewis, P. (eds) *The Sociology of the Professions*. London: Macmillan.
Johnson, T.L. (1972) *Professions and Power*. London: Macmillan.
Johnson, T.L. (1984) 'Professionalism: Occupation or ideology?' In Goodlad, S. (ed.) *Education for Professions*. Guildford: SRHE/NFER/Nelson.
Parsons, T. (1968) 'Professions'. In Sills, D. (ed.) *The International Encyclopedia of the Social Sciences*, **11**, 536–47. New York: Macmillan and Free Press.
Polytechnics and Colleges Funding Council (1990) *Profiles of Polytechnics and Colleges*. London: PCFC.
Waddington, I. (1985) 'Professions'. In Kuper, A. and Kuper, J. (eds) *Social Science Encyclopedia*. London: Routledge & Kegan Paul.
Watson, D. (1989) *Managing the Modular Course*. Milton Keynes: SRHE/Open University Press.

2

Issues in Course Design

Hazel Bines

The context of course design

As noted in Chapter 1, several key influences are currently shaping the
education of the professions in higher education. Each of these in turn has
a range of implications for course design. In particular, there are considerable demands for course innovation, resulting from developments in professional requirements and practices. Professional education is also subject
to the pressures on resources currently being experienced by all forms of
higher education, within an academic culture which, as noted in Chapter
1, still tends to celebrate the primacy of 'pure' and 'hard' science, specialist
rather than interdisciplinary work, and research rather than teaching
(Becher, 1989).

At the same time, there are a number of exciting developments in course
design and delivery. Moreover, although the heterogeneity which character-
izes the professions means that pressures and expectations may vary, there
are a number of common issues, including the role of professional education
in developing professional competence, models and methodologies of
professional education, partnership with the professional community, and
making the most effective use of available resources. However, many of
these issues are difficult to resolve. For example, although the main aim of
professional education would seem to be self-evident, in that such courses
are primarily concerned with developing competent practitioners (Jarvis,
1983), this is, as Jarvis notes, somewhat over-simplistic. The definition of
competence, tensions between liberal and vocational conceptions of education, finding the most effective design and delivery and differences along
the spectrum of professional development, from pre-service education to
that for in-service and continuing professional development (CPD), are all
problematic. In addition, as noted in Chapter 1, course design for most
professions is increasingly being undertaken in the context of a range of
different and possibly conflicting interests. These include: the interests of
those concerned with the supply and quality of professional services, such

as employers, voluntary agencies, the state and consumers of professional services; the interests of the professional community in relation to identity, status and resources; the interests of higher education, including questions of teaching, research and resources; and finally, the interests of both the educators themselves and their students (cf. Goodlad, 1984). The two key questions in course design, concerning the aims of a course and how these should be realized, are thus likely to involve a number of complex factors. Aims may range from competence and accreditation to student and service consumer needs and the realization of those aims may include not only models and methods but also the possibilities and constraints engendered by available resources.

To date, professional education has approached such questions in a number of ways, thus providing a final aspect of the context of course design, namely the historical legacy of particular models and their in-fluence on current practice. Past and current models encompass most of the current debate about professional education course design and will thus now be discussed.

Models of professional education

To date there have been three main models of professional education, as summarized in Table 2.1.[1] The first can be characterized as the 'appren-ticeship' or 'pre-technocratic' model. Professional education takes place largely on the job but some instruction may be given through block and/or day release in an associated training school or institute of further or higher education. The curriculum largely comprises the acquisition of 'cookbook' knowledge embodied in practice manuals and the mastery of practical routines. Instruction is largely provided by experienced practition-ers, although subject specialists may make a contribution, either to liberal-ize the curriculum or to make specified and strictly limited contributions on particular knowledge elements. This is primarily a model for initial rather than continuing professional development, characterized by a tight and instrumental focus on professional requirements and competences which are not seen as problematic. Such specifications are largely externally de-termined, for both course providers and course participants, in terms of curriculum and assessment, by employers or national quangos or some combination of the two.

The second model, called here the 'technocratic' model, has become the pattern of professional education for a large number of professions in recent years. It has tended to take place in schools associated with, or incorporated in, institutions of higher education. It is characterized by the division of professional education into three main elements. The first com-prises the development and transmission of a systematic knowledge base, largely, though not exclusively, based on contributing academic disciplines, such as the natural and social sciences, including both 'pure' and 'applied' dimensions. The second involves the interpretation and application of the knowledge base to practice, including coverage of the range of professional activities and their contexts, problem-solving principles and processes and socialization into particular values and behaviours. Presentation is often multidisciplinary and/or may be based on theoretical models of practice, for example, 'the nursing process' in nurse education. The third element is the supervised practice in selected placements (Schein, 1972; Schön, 1987). This model also represents a shift in control towards the educational institutions who run the courses. Employer and national bodies may select and accredit institutions and their courses and may be involved in course design and validation. However, curriculum content and delivery are largely the responsibility of course providers, who also usually play the dominant role in the final assessment of professional competence.

The model is, however, regarded as having some serious weaknesses. Although it can be regarded as being liberal as well as instrumental in aim, in that the student's personal as well as professional education is included (for example through developing knowledge of one or more academic disciplines), there may be considerable variations in concepts of professional competence, the knowledge base transmitted, approaches to teaching both theory and practice and degrees of student choice. These may arise from differing concepts of the particular profession and also the high degree of institutional autonomy involved. Secondly, it can easily fragment overall learning into discrete and unrelated parts, including a disjunction between theory and practice. It also tends to lead to sharp divisions of labour in teaching, between specialists in the academic disciplines in question, academics concerned with theories and models for practice (normally former practitioners with appropriate academic and teaching credentials) and those involved in placements (who are normally experienced practitioners employed in the relevant professional service or organization rather than by the higher education institution). Above all, the practice element is marginalized or of low status, even when rhetorically put forward as a major or culminating element of the course.

Most importantly, however, this model is based on what Schön (1983, 1987) has described as 'technical rationality', that is a view of both professionalism and professional education which fails to reflect the nature of professional knowledge and action and the ways in which professionals actually develop their practice. Most professional activity is based not on the two-step application of knowledge to practice but on an integrated knowledge-in-action, much of which is spontaneous and tacit. Moreover, real-world practice is primarily made up of messy and indeterminate situations and unique cases, often involving conflicts of values, which practitioners cannot simply resolve through applying theories or techniques from their existing store of professional technical knowledge. Practitioners solve the demands of both the routine and the more problematic requirements of practice through a continuous process of reflection in and on action, an 'artistry' of practice. The knowledge and techniques of technical rationality,

Table 2.1 Models of professional education

Model	What	Where	Who	Accountability
Pre-technocratic 'apprenticeship' model	Practical routines. 'Cookbook' knowledge embodied in practice manuals. Mastery of facts, routines, and place in hierarchy of authority are key elements in learning and assessment.	On-the-job or in job-related training school. Block or day release common for 'theoretical' instruction.	Experienced practitioners as instructors. Producers of manuals for practice. Subject specialists either to liberalize curriculum or contribute specified and restricted elements to course/manual.	Educational institutions' control over character and content of their contribution to training is severely restricted. Employer-dominated learning or national curriculum and examinations. Role of subject specialist limited and subordinate. Accountable through course organizer to employer or national board.
Technocratic model	1. Systematic knowledge base which legitimates claims to autonomy, status and closure in complex division of labour. 2. Interpretation and application of knowledge base to practice. Multi-	In schools associated with higher education. Academic education may precede professional school which dominates Phases 2 and 3, or schools incorporated in higher education institutions and draw on academic departments for Phase 1.	Academic subject specialists. + Former practitioners with appropriate academic credentials who direct courses and specialize in interpreting and applying selected academic insights to development of	Educational institutions' control over character and content of professional education and training is predominant. Within educational institutions uneasy battles over rigour versus relevance between subject specialists and

	disciplinary, holistic, and involving values as well as knowledge – often termed 'principles and practice' and involves development of theories or models for practice. 3. Supervised practice in workplace.	Patterns and degree of integration vary synchronically and diachronically.	theoretical base for practice. + Supervisors, tutors in practice.	professional tutors. Practice supervisors/tutors subordinate in educational role to professional college-based tutors and often lower status and pay.
Post-technocratic model	Knowledge for practice. Growing emphasis on acquisition of professional competences. Theories-in-use of most competent and effective practitioners. Development of systematic reflection on practice and acquisition of 'research' skills required to use reflection, observation, analysis and evaluation to develop practice.	'Practicum' is key place where competence to practice is developed and comes to dominate curriculum. Organized in different ways in different occupations.	Subject specialist eliminated, or negotiated role based on professional credibility acquired through research. Professional tutors in partnership with practitioner-educators who operate in 'schools' as well as in practice setting. Practitioner-educator becomes dominant figure and style of supervision changes to promote reflective practice.	Partnership between higher education and employing agency, through contract learning.

Source: Peter George

that is science and research, are thus bounded and mediated by the arts of problem-framing, implementation and improvisation (Schön, ibid.). It therefore follows that the best preparation for practice will involve primary emphasis being given to a 'practicum' within which students can be initiated into the customs, methods and working practices of the profession, by senior, competent practitioners (Schön, ibid.).

The recognition, by some professional educators at least, of the weaknesses of the technocratic model, together with other factors such as continuing political and social concern over the ineffectiveness of professions, have led to the development of a third model, which can be characterized as the 'post-technocratic' model. It is not yet a coherent or fully developed model, but it does include particular features, in particular the emphasis on the acquisition of professional competences. Such competences are primarily developed through experience of practice and reflection on practice in a practicum within which students have access to skilled practitioners who act as coaches. Such a practicum may be institution- or employment-based (or both) and provides a bridge between the academic institution and the world of practice and between professional education and subsequent employment.

The practicum is thus the key and integrating element of the course and the professional education tutor and the practice tutor become major educational figures. In addition, course elements outside of the practicum will also primarily focus on issues of professional practice, with cognate disciplines being integrated, contextualized and utilized in the study and development of the competences, settings and problems of professional practice. There is also a greater emphasis on individual student learning and progress and on a partnership of higher education institutions, services and employers.

However, despite these common features, the model has a number of potentially disparate elements, due to both continuing differences of opinion and practice within professions and professional education, and the particular political, social and educational contexts within which the model is currently being developed. Thus in some versions of this model, the majority of attention has been given to the identification and description of a range of discrete competences, largely described in behavioural terms, which are then developed and assessed, primarily through a practice setting (Tuxworth, 1989). Other approaches, while stressing the importance of the practicum, do not concentrate so much on discrete competences as on the general development of a capacity for critical reflection in and on action, as the key to continuing professional growth (McNamara, 1990).

Although this new model is increasingly becoming the pattern of professional education, it brings a number of new challenges, not least the need to further develop our knowledge of the range of competences involved in a particular profession, an understanding of how students do acquire professional competence, how skilled teaching can enable them to do so and what are the best settings for this learning to take place. There may also be some major difficulties in reconciling epistemologically distinct aspects of the model, namely the largely positivist, behaviourist approaches which have engendered the current 'competency movement' and the interpretive theories of human thinking and action which underpin the concept of 'reflection'. There are also a number of new issues which need to be resolved, for example ensuring that course design and delivery does enable the integration of knowledge and action, making the practicum effective, constructing new partnerships between higher education, employers and services and facilitating student choice. In addition, and reflecting the long-standing neglect of continuing professional development within professional education, most attention has been given to the implementation of this model for initial or pre-service training. Nevertheless, it does offer ways of resolving some of the dilemmas and credibility of professional education to date, in that it requires the articulation of professional competence and attempts to integrate the different elements of professional education around what most would regard as its central core: the development of professional practice. The next section will therefore consider some of the particular issues which now need to be resolved, including competences, the role of the practicum and the development of new training partnerships, together with implications for course design. Reflecting current trends, this section will focus on initial training, before moving to discuss continuing professional development.

Developing the post-technocratic model

Competence

Although the current debate on competence often implies that this is a fairly new approach to education and training, including professional education, issues of competence are at the heart of a long-standing debate about what professionalism entails, including the debate about technical rationality, artistry and reflection outlined earlier. However, the practice of using qualifications rather than a profile of competences as entry to employment has meant that competence has been implicitly rather than explicitly addressed, and traditional course design has focused more on levels, structures and content than on detailed specifications of the skills, knowledge and experience required by particular professionals and how these will be developed. In addition, the tendency of research on professions to focus on issues, clientele and contexts, rather than on the nature of professional action itself, has resulted in a lack of information on which to base an explicit focus on competence. Thus it has become only too easy to suggest, as Burke (1989) and others have done, that current professional education needs the 'competency movement' to make it effective. However, despite some of the claims of the competency advocates, adopting a competency approach in itself will not provide every solution to the weaknesses of current professional education. Three major issues need to be resolved, namely what is meant by the general notion of competence, what are the competences involved in a particular profession and thirdly, how are they best developed and assessed?

Athough the term 'competence' is now in wide use, there would seem to be little agreement about what it comprises in practice. The definition put forward by the Training Agency, for example, and on which much current developmental work in the UK is now based,[2] is a wide one, including organization and planning of work, innovation, coping with non-routine activities and interpersonal effectiveness (TA, 1988). However it is basically concerned with the ability to *perform* the activities within an occupation (TA, ibid.) and is thus fundamentally behavioural in conception, even though knowledge as well as skills may be assessed and particular competences may vary from a single task to a highly complex set of activities. Moreover, the assumption that a specific set of competences can be identified for a particular profession is based on a technical–rational conception of professionalism, even though the focus may have moved from the science and applied science relevant to a particular profession to the nature of professional action itself. In seeking to establish a set of ordered and universal competences, this approach no more easily admits the messy indeterminate zones of practice and the unique, value-laden nature of many professional problems (Schön, op. cit.) than did earlier versions of technical rationality. It may thus be both epistemologically and heuristically incompatible with a view which centres on the development of reflection and experience, including the artistry which is at the heart of Schön's reconceptualization of professional action and education.

At the same time, the new focus on professional competence does have considerable potential for developing the post-technocratic model, in that it is primarily concerned with professional knowledge and professional action, rather than cognate disciplines, and thus both gives credence to professional practice and emphasizes the centrality of the practicum. And although Schön's critique and conception of professional action and education does perhaps create a dichotomy between science and artistry (Schulman, 1988), the role of technical knowledge and understanding is certainly not dismissed – just given a more limited place, with artistry mediating, rather than being excluded by, applied science and technique (Schön, 1987, p. 13). Given that most professions continue to lack the detailed understanding of professional action to make professional education really effective, a focus on competence should considerably enhance both the rigour and the relevance of professional education. As Zeichner has noted in relation to the education of teachers (a profession with a particularly weak conception of, and research tradition on, professional action), the issue is not the exclusive validity of two competing paradigms but utilizing what each has to contribute (Zeichner, 1990). It may therefore be possible, as illustrated by the case studies in this chapter, to develop a broad vision of competence involving both behavioural and interpretive approaches.

Course design must also address the specific nature of the competences of a particular profession, taking into consideration that such competences are very likely to be both contested and contestable, dependent as they are on a range of possibly competing definitions of the professional role and of 'good practice' as well as on a range of professional and other interests within the professional community, higher education and society. Most course design is likely to have to meet the competences identified and defined by professional accrediting bodies. However these may not represent the views of other professionals or of the educators involved in the particular course, which may lead to a number of problems in terms of both aims and content. 'Competency' is thus not an easy solution to issues of course aims and design. Nevertheless such problems must be resolved since competency is increasingly likely to provide the conceptual framework within which the aims, and the subsequent design and delivery of courses, will be set.

Course integration

It has already been noted that the post-technocratic model may well involve a move away from what Bernstein (1971) has characterized as a 'collection code', with strong boundaries between subjects or disciplines, towards an 'integrated code' which will bring together the academic and professional elements of courses through an increasingly explicit focus on the development of professional competence.[3] Thus, instead of students largely making their own links between pure or applied knowledge and professional practice, such connections will be deliberately structured as an integral part of the course design. However, as will be discussed later in more detail in this and other chapters in this book, it is not easy to develop course elements which both develop professional knowledge and understanding and also do justice to the substantive and methodological concerns of contributing disciplines, or to integrate 'theory' and 'practice' and in particular, institution-based course elements, with the experiences of the practicum. Such integration also requires a closer partnership between subject and professional tutors and between the higher education institution and the employers and services involved in the practicum.

Course integration also raises questions endemic to all forms of course design, including progression, differentiation, choice and organization. For example, the focus on specific professional competences is likely to mean that core, compulsory elements will form a large part of any course. The complex process of learning to be increasingly competent in the different aspects of professional action will require considerable attention to issues of progression, through a course design which either sequences competences in order of difficulty, or more likely, a spiral curriculum which will return several times to the same forms of professional action and problems, but with increasingly demanding and complex expectations of student knowledge and skill. However, as Cork (1987) has noted in relation to nursing education, a spiral approach may not always be appropriate, either because of the lack of time, or the range of disciplines involved, or because the nature of the knowledge is more suited to other forms of sequencing, such as structural logic or chronology. Sequencing must also allow for differences in the pace or depth of student progress, to ensure that the acceptable minimum (and preferably more than minimum) level of competence is finally achieved.

Such pressures on the curriculum inevitably have an impact on student choice, an issue which is becoming increasingly important in the light of the development of new approaches to credit and to modes of learning. These developments, especially when allied to a competence-based approach to course design, also raise further questions about course integration. It has been argued, for example, in relation to National Vocational Qualifications (NVQs), that statements of competence are independent of any course or programme of learning and may be achieved through experiential, workplace and open learning as well as more formal programmes of education and training (Jessup, 1989). Although this will undoubtedly increase access, flexibility, choice and partnerships between education and the workplace, it could lead to fragmentation of the learning process. It also underestimates how professional education engenders socialization into a professional culture and identity, in particular the acquisition of attitudes and values. Finally, it neglects the powerful and integrative support of the peer group and of staff who know students and the course well, and can structure learning experiences and the learning environment in ways which are conducive and supportive to both the aims and organization of the course and the needs of individuals (Youll, 1985).

Nevertheless, as particularly discussed by McDougall and by Robertson later in this chapter, course design for professional education will in future have to take account of credit accumulation and transfer schemes (CATS), the accreditation of experiential and work-based learning and the mix of modes of learning which students may choose to follow.[4] The most common form of response to such issues has been modularization, which can provide particular flexibility in relation to credit and to choice of learning modes and programmes. Certainly, as noted in Chapter 1, our own experience at Oxford Polytechnic, in relation to a large and long-established modular course, suggests that professional education can be effectively delivered in such a framework. Modules or units can be developed for integrated and discrete course content, and the practicum, and membership of a modular framework facilitates access to a range of academic and professional modules and staff. However, particular attention needs to be given to the balance of the philosophy of modularity – for example, choice and flexibility – with the particular requirements of professional courses in terms of compulsory study, course integration and student support and progression (CNAA, 1990a). Modularity also requires effective systems of information and resource management (Watson *et al.*, 1989). Thus although, like competence, modularity is increasingly likely to frame course design for professional education, its value and effectiveness should be carefully monitored.

Developing the practicum

Despite its new centrality to professional education, and a long tradition of providing practice placements, including sandwich placements, the practicum remains the least developed element of most courses. However, as Zeichner, has noted, in comments on teacher education which are nevertheless applicable to most professional education, the practicum can no longer be left as an unmediated or unstructured experience, not only because of its importance to student learning but also because of political and resource pressures to return to some form of apprenticeship model.[5] He argues that attention needs to be given to three aspects of change in the practicum experience, namely organizational (e.g. length and location), curricular (what is to be learned and how) and structural (including both the resources supplied to support the practicum and the contextual conditions in which it exists) (Zeichner, op. cit., p. 107).

In relation to organization, it is likely that the practicum will increase in both length and frequency and that although a role may remain for the simulated practice setting, the practicum will be primarily located in actual workplaces, in order to foster professional competence. This may well put pressure on the time available for course components within the higher education institution element of a course, in particular the time given to relevant disciplines, even within an integrated or thematic approach. The curriculum of the practicum will thus become increasingly important, both because of its role in learning and to compensate for the loss of time elsewhere. For these reasons, and because of the complexity of professional roles and settings, practica are thus likely to be designed around a set of specific and sequenced tasks, activities and experiences, closely related to other course elements through supervision, tutorials, seminars and written assignments (see Glenny and Hickling, below). The development of professional competence, and in particular reflection, will require course design to explicitly foster particular methods of teaching and learning, such as observation, modelling, routine practice, problem solving and evaluation, each of which will be undertaken in partnership with the experienced practitioners involved.

However, these new requirements for the practicum are taking place in a context where the traditional marginalization of work placements in higher education is being exacerbated by increasing resource constraints (Zeichner, ibid.). This, coupled with pressures on many practitioners from innovation and cuts in services or both, may well shape the nature of the practicum and will certainly have an impact on the support available to realize its objectives. The role of the practicum, the effective deployment of available resources and integration with other course elements are thus likely to be major issues in future course design.

Constructing new partnerships

The development of the practicum will be one specific arena of a developing partnership between higher education, employers and services. Other aspects of such partnerships with particular implications for course design include the new approaches to credit and the growing involvement of practitioners in the processes of course development, validation, accreditation and review.[6] This shift in control away from higher education is part of the growing emphasis on professional competence and the importance of the practicum. However despite the willingness of many higher education institutions and employing/placement services to enter into partnership, neither funding nor training is necessarily available to develop either the role of the practice teacher/professional mentor within the practicum or the contribution of practising professionals to a course as a whole. Similar points can be made about the resources and opportunities available to support contributions from higher education towards the development of work-based or open learning programmes. Both the processes and the outcomes of course design are thus based on considerable professional goodwill and commitment which could be considered to be neither appropriate nor entirely secure.

Finally, course design now also presumes an increasing partnership with the student, who may both choose a range of options in relation to programmes and modes of learning and who also has to be seen as increasingly autonomous and responsible in relation to his or her professional development towards competence.[7] In addition, although all these aspects of partnership are relevant to pre-service education, they are particularly salient in relation to continuing professional development (CPD).

Continuing professional development

Discussion to date in this chapter, and in professional education in general, has largely centred on initial or pre-service professional education. However, it is increasingly recognized that CPD is an equally crucial element, with particular implications for course design (Houle, 1980; Todd, 1987). Social, economic and technological change, and issues of standards and quality assurance, all require greater attention to the process of maintaining, improving and extending professional competence throughout a professional's working life (Welsh and Woodward, 1989). To date, CPD provision has tended to comprise workshops and conferences, courses (including distance learning) and more recently, employment-based staff development and appraisal. Unlike initial professional education, responsibility for CPD has been largely that of employers, and to a lesser extent, professional bodies, or more often than not has been left to individuals wishing to improve career prospects. Perhaps because labour supply, at least until recently, has not been a major issue, large-scale government funding, through courses in higher education institutions, is still rare, although many such institutions work collaboratively with employers and professional bodies and provide most of the award-bearing courses for individuals.

In CPD there is also a more explicit concern with the immediate or long-term needs of the service or industry as well as the individual's professional development. The response of higher education has either been 'market-led', typically in response to a 'one-off' request, or has comprised the weakly marketed (though often well-subscribed) provider-led course, reflecting the particular interests and expertise of the institution concerned. The market-led course has largely addressed updating or development of employer-determined, precisely defined knowledge and competences (the master professional variant of the apprenticeship model) whilst the provider-led course has often reflected the approach of the technocratic model, for example by offering an extension of knowledge of cognate disciplines and professional theory, rarely with a practice element, not necessarily linked to students' current professional responsibilities and often including a research project or dissertation, similar to that of the traditional, academic, post-graduate course.

However, similarly to pre-service professional education, changes external to the professions, together with concern about professional credibility and competence, have now fostered a post-technocratic model for CPD courses, focusing on the development of professional competence, though with reference to the demands made on the experienced and often more senior professional. In addition to updating of various elements of technical and professional knowledge, there is often an emphasis on policy analysis and implementation, problem-solving and general management skills. Although professional requirements and context may differ, the issues already discussed in relation to the design of initial qualification courses are very similar. They include: the need to identify and articulate the range of competences required of the experienced professional; the difficulties of integrating discipline-based and profession-based theory; and developing and integrating the practicum, in this case through the student's current professional post.

Many courses now focus on the range of policies and practical problems encountered by working professional students, utilizing knowledge and methods in problem-solving processes, and linking to professional practice through a project or action research. Such approaches not only reflect a serious attempt to ensure a core focus on professional activity but are also attractive to professionals with little time for academic study divorced from their working concerns. Simultaneously, they have the potential to help solve service or industry needs through the medium of individual development (see McDougall, below, and Gaunt, Chapter 4). In addition, customization of courses, and accreditation of employment-based learning (see Robertson, below, and Hughes, Chapter 3) can facilitate the construction of the partnership between employers and educators identified earlier as a significant element of new approaches to initial professional education.

Such an approach makes a number of demands on staff in higher education. As well as the requirement for a high standard of up-to-date professional knowledge and credibility, in the context of increasing and changing credentialism, there is a particular need for flexibility in delivery modes in order to accommodate part-time students, particular employer and individual needs and choice, a mix of open and institution-based learning, and credit accumulation and transfer (including credit for prior experiential and work-based learning). Modularity is again providing a major solution to such issues (CNAA, 1990b; Gaunt, Chapter 4) although the maintenance of both choice and sufficient specialism in the more market-led environment of CPD can put considerable pressure on resources for delivery which need to be considered as an aspect of course design (Glasson, Chapter 4). In addition, issues of teaching, learning, assessment and the learning environment, which will be considered in Chapter 3, and which are important elements in all course design, need particular consideration in relation to CPD. Nevertheless, CPD courses are likely to become a growing aspect of provision, reflecting and sharpening many of the trends and issues in pre-service education and professional education as a whole.

Conclusion

Course design for professional education thus involves the most effective use of structures, content, methods and human and material resources to realize a range of aims related to definitions of professional competences, beliefs about the nature of professional and other education, the importance of the practicum, demands for the accreditation of a range of forms of learning, the needs/stage of the professional concerned, and relationships between various academics, professionals, students, employers and services. The case studies below illustrate these many facets of course design. Ruth Champion considers both the philosophy of a nursing degree and the consequences of that philosophy for course content, the practicum, partnership with a service and staffing. Glen McDougall continues the focus on operational but reflective practice, and as well as considering issues of interdisciplinary work and the various interests involved in professional education, including consumer rights, identifies how modularity (unit credit), flexibility in modes of delivery and particular teaching approaches can fulfil both initial and CPD student needs. Georgina Glenny and Elizabeth Hickling give further consideration to the design and integration of the practicum. They consider both institution and work-based practica and in looking at teacher education, discuss how courses can draw on student experience, deal with the complexities of professional roles and settings and provide a range of structured activities within practica. The theme of different interests in professional education is further illustrated in Denise Morrey's account of the processes involved in designing a course for accreditation by a professional body. Finally, Clive Robertson elaborates the issues of credit and partnership with employers through discussion of the accreditation of company training programmes.

Above all, however, the complex nature of the issues and processes involved in these case studies, and in the preceding discussion in this chapter, indicate that institutions should – and can – facilitate and support course development in a variety of ways, including: fostering debate about models of professional education; providing advice on aspects of course design; disseminating information across professional courses and areas about possible solutions to particular problems; and developing frameworks for courses and for credit arrangements, such as modular schemes, CAT schemes, and protocols and systems for the accreditation of experiential and employment-based learning. In addition, institutions can support negotiations with professional bodies in relation to course accreditation and encourage and facilitate partnerships with employers and services. Without precluding initiative and creativity, or the inevitable differences between professions and particular courses or programmes, a progressive approach to course design, and an acknowledgement of particular requirements and constraints, including both academic and resource implications, would do much to further develop effective courses and remedy some of the cultural, political and material difficulties faced by professional education within higher education. The issues and solutions involved in course design for professional education demonstrate how far it is initiating developments which are relevant to all courses within higher education: the potential and actual contribution of such education to institutional development as a whole now needs to be fully acknowledged, utilized and supported.

Notes

1. I would like to acknowledge the major contribution of Peter George, one of the other authors in this book, to this section on models of professional education, in particular his permission to reproduce his diagram as Table 2.1 and to use ideas and extracts from some of his unpublished papers in relation to the typology of the three models described. In addition, I would like to thank him for his helpful and thoughtful comments on earlier drafts of the whole chapter.
2. It informs, for example, the development of NVQs, including potential development at Level 5 (degree level). Burke (1989) provides a number of useful summaries of the development of competency-based education in the UK and USA, and Robins and Webster (1989) provide both analysis and critique of the particular FEU/MSC approach.
3. The systematic application of Bernstein's (1971) analysis to professional education would be both useful and illuminating since Bernstein also links particular codes to particular forms of framing – teaching, learning, assessment and control. Bernstein's analysis also suggests that although an integrated code may appear to foster more student autonomy, it may exercise a more subtle and pervasive form of control (cf. Robins and Webster, op. cit.).
4. There is now a growing literature on CATS, APEL and open learning. See for example, Bennett and McGoldrick (1988), CNAA (1990c) and Evans (1988).

5. For example, critics of teacher education are suggesting that courses be replaced with 'training on the job', with the 'licensed teacher', that is someone with two years of higher education who is then appointed to a school, and trained there, possibly supported by some input from teacher education institutions, being one outcome to date of such a policy.
6. For example, it is common practice for CNAA courses to have practising professionals or representatives from business/industry on both course planning committees and validation/review panels. However, as Morrey notes below, professional bodies remain very influential.
7. See note 3.

References

Becher, T. (1989) *Academic Tribes and Territories.* Milton Keynes: SRHE/Open University.
Bennett, Y. and McGoldrick, C. (1988) *Open Learning in Polytechnics and Colleges of Higher Education.* Huddersfield Polytechnic/MSC.
Bernstein, B. (1971) 'The classification and framing of educational knowlege'. In Young, M.F.D. (ed.) *Knowledge and Control.* London: Macmillan.
Burke, J. (1989) (ed.) *Competency Based Education and Training.* Lewes: The Falmer Press.
CNAA (1990a) *Complex Modular Inservice Education Schemes: A Review of CNAA Provision.* London: CNAA.
CNAA (1990b) *The Modular Option.* London: CNAA.
CNAA (1990c) *CNAA Handbook 1990–91.* London: CNAA.
Cork, N.M. (1987) 'Approaches to curriculum planning'. In Davis, B. (ed.) *Nursing Education: Research and Developments.* London: Croom Helm.
Evans, N. (1988) *The Assessment of Prior Experiential Learning.* London: CNAA.
Goodlad, S. (1984) 'Introduction'. In Goodlad, S. (ed.) *Education for the Professions.* Guildford: SRHE/NFER-Nelson.
Houle, C. (1980) *Continuing Learning in the Professions.* San Francisco: Jossey-Bass.
Jarvis, P. (1983) *Professional Education.* London: Croom Helm.
Jessup, G. (1989) 'The emerging model of vocational education and training'. In Burke, J. (ed.) *Competency Based Education and Training.* Lewes: The Falmer Press.
McNamara, D. (1990) 'Research on teachers' thinking: its contribution to educating student teachers to think critically'. *Journal of Education for Teaching,* **16**(2), 147–60.
Robins, K. and Webster, F. (1989) *The Technical Fix.* London: Macmillan.
Schein, E.H. (1972) *Professional Education: Some New Directions.* New York: McGraw-Hill/Carnegie Foundation.
Schön, D.A. (1983) *The Reflective Practitioner.* London: Temple Smith.
Schön, D.A. (1987) *Educating the Reflective Practitioner.* London: Jossey-Bass.
Schulman, L.S. (1988) 'The dangers of dichotomous thinking in education'. In Grimmett, P. and Erikson, E. (eds) *Reflection in Teacher Education.* New York: Pacific Educational Press.
Todd, F. (1987) (ed.) *Planning Continuing Professional Development.* London: Croom Helm.
Training Agency (Employment Department) (1988) *Employment for the 1990s* (Cm. 540). London: HMSO.

Tuxworth, E. (1989) 'Competence based education and training: Background and origins'. In Burke, J. (ed.) *Competency Based Education and Training.* Lewes: The Falmer Press.

Watson, D. (1989) *Managing the Modular Course.* Milton Keynes: SRHE/Open University Press.

Welsh, L. and Woodward, P. (1989) *Continuing Professional Development: Towards a National Strategy.* London: FEU/DES (PICKUP).

Youll, P. (1985) 'The learning community'. In Harris, R.J. (ed.) *Educating Social Workers.* Leicester: Association of Teachers in Social Work Education.

Zeichner, K. (1990) 'Changing directions in the practicum; looking ahead to the 1990s'. *Journal of Education for Teaching,* **16**(2), 105–32.

CASE STUDIES

The Philosophy of an Honours Degree Programme in Nursing and Midwifery

Ruth Champion

The degree programme which is the focus of this case study is unique in terms of the nature of the partnership between the Polytechnic and the health authority concerned. This account identifies the central tenets upon which the development was based and traces its translation through course design to the initial stages of implementation.

The programme comprises four Honours degrees in nursing (general adults, children's, mental health and mental handicap) and a degree in midwifery, all of which lead to registration as a nurse or midwife. It has replaced the traditional training programmes in the health authority. Key features include the philosophy of the programme, its links with thinking and developments in nursing and midwifery practice, and the centrality of practice, which last has resulted in nearly half of the teaching staff being practice-based.

The programme planning was initiated by nursing, midwifery practitioners, managers and educators. Although thinking developed concurrently with the nursing education reform proposals of *Project 2000* (UKCC, 1985), change was not exclusively a response to this, nor was planning imposed by education on practice. From the start therefore, the nursing and midwifery service owned the planning as much as the School of Nursing or the Polytechnic, and these three groups were represented in all planning structures. These included the formal committees dealing with overall policy, with course planning, with organizational and resource issues and with staff development, as well as small groups working on specific aspects of the curriculum.

The philosophy of the programme was the subject of early and ongoing discussion and may be summarized under four headings:

- beliefs about nursing and midwifery
- beliefs about becoming a professional practitioner
- beliefs about knowledge in nursing and midwifery
- beliefs about student learning.

Each of these will be briefly discussed, indicating the nature of the beliefs and how they were translated into course design and initial implementation.

Beliefs about nursing and midwifery

These beliefs centre on nursing and midwifery as essentially an interpersonal activity concerned with promoting health and the capacity of individuals or groups to cope with a change in their health status, such as illness or disability. The focus of nursing is seen as shifting from an illness-oriented, physical activity towards a health-oriented, interpersonal, supportive, educative process. This thinking reflects the emphasis in *Project 2000* (UKCC, ibid.) and other reports, for example, the World Health Organization *Targets for Health for All by the Year 2000* (WHO, 1985). The shift in focus also enables students of the four branches of nursing (general adult, children's, mental health and mental handicap) to study together and with midwifery students, particularly in the early stages of their programme, before specializing. The emphasis also underlines nursing and midwifery as making unique contributions to health care, complementary to, and interdependent with, medicine.

In curricular terms, previously separate linear programmes thus come together for the first half of the course. Initial studies include: debates about the nature of health; exploration of the nature of health; and discussion of factors influencing health. Instead of early immersion in institutional care, students undertake studies on their own health profile, link with a family who are well and study a neighbourhood from the perspective of health.

This early work enables students to place all future experience with people who have a particular need for health care, whether they be pregnant, disturbed, physically ill or disabled, in the context of understanding the complexity of, and variants in, health. Health promotional and educative activities thus become as important a part of the nursing repertoire as, for example, assisting a person to wash, giving medication or encouraging people to express their fears about their illness or anger about their situation.

The curricular challenge comes not so much in the complete reshaping of the syllabus (i.e. putting health, people, families and community caring before illness or disturbance, hospitals and procedures) but in maintaining the health promotion theme in later parts of the course when students are working in more traditional settings. Staff in these settings are used to working within their specialism and have not necessarily fully developed a health orientation. For example, they may not see the benefit of a student linking with a patient prior to admission, and then following them through admission, treatment and discharge. Such a 'follow-through' experience however, may help students to understand the nature of support needed by patients in hospital to prepare them to resume responsibility for their own health care on discharge. The maintenance of a health emphasis through-out the course will therefore be one aspect of course monitoring.

Beliefs about becoming a professional practitioner

An examination of the outcome of previous patterns of course organization (e.g. Bendall, 1975; Hunt, 1979; Orton, 1981; Fretwell, 1982; Ogier, 1982; Melia, 1987) led key figures in the course team to conclude that the centres of learning about professional practice are not classrooms. They are the places where professional practice takes place, such as people's homes, health centres, residential hostels, community hospitals, and hospital wards and departments. Supported by the work of Schön (1983, 1987) on the nature of professional practice, and Benner (1984) who examined the nature of developing expertise in nurses, the course team adopted a 'reflective practice' model of professional education. This emphasizes the centrality of practice to professional education and requires both expert professionals and students to make explicit the decisions they are making, through re-flection and analysis of real situations. In recognizing the academic value of practice, the programmes thus reject the traditional view within higher education (particularly medical schools) that the 'hard, high ground' (Schön, 1983) of ascribed scientific thinking should underpin the whole of profes-sional practice. Instead it is recognized that such practice is centrally concerned with a response to unique situations which are not subject to the rigorous controls of scientific enquiry.

The statutory regulations for nursing courses in the European Community require a programme of 4600 curricular hours, of which the English National Board for Nursing, Midwifery and Health Visitors requires half to be designated for learning within practice settings (ENB, 1989). Traditional nursing programmes have complied with such requirements through an 'apprenticeship' model (see Bines, above), within which student nurses have spent far more than the minimum hours in care giving, most of this in the role of a worker. The early syllabuses of training focused on 'recipe' nursing procedures and on knowledge of diseases and disorders. During the 1970s, under North American influence, the concept of nursing as 'problem-solving', 'research-based' and requiring systematic assessment, planning and evaluation began to be explored (DHSS, 1972; Kratz, 1979;

Crow, 1980; Roper *et al.*, 1980). This technical–rational approach (Schön, 1983; Bines, above) was particularly adopted by the small number of under-graduate nursing courses based in universities and polytechnics (Owen, 1984).

The course team wished to retain this enquiring, analytic approach but believed that the analysis of practice should be centred in practice. One outcome of this thinking was the development of the role of 'lecturer prac-titioner' – expert practitioners who would be responsible for the 50 per cent of the course that was practice-based (see Champion, Chapter 4). With nearly half of the staff for the course being based in practice, the result has been a 'practice-driven' course, with practitioners who are fully education-ally accountable taking responsibility for the theoretical input related to nursing or midwifery practice, as well as supervision, discussion and analysis of that practice. Thus the statement of the nursing and midwifery statutory body, that practice must be educationally led (ENB, op. cit.), has been turned into a practice-led process of education.

Beliefs about knowledge in nursing and midwifery

It is widely recognized that knowledge used in nursing and midwifery is drawn from a range of disciplines including psychology, sociology, biologi-cal and medical science and ethics (Smith, 1981; Chapman, 1985). Know-ledge from these areas, together with the developing body of health, nursing and midwifery knowledge and studies, is combined and used in practice (Dickoff and James, 1968; Smith op. cit.). In the apprenticeship form of nurse training, the nature of the knowledge taught was not made explicit. A key feature of undergraduate programmes, including this case study, is the recognition not only of the source and subject bases of knowl-edge but also its dynamic nature. A consequent assumption of our courses is that only those who are knowledgeable in a subject will undertake its teaching. Moreover, it is assumed that they will be responsible for those specific subject inputs in terms of developing and delivering the syllabus, assessing students' performance and evaluating learning experiences.

Although this is the general pattern in higher education, it has not been so evident in Schools of Nursing, where staff have tended to teach a pre-determined syllabus and assessments have been drawn from a bank of ques-tions, marked by a panel of teachers on a rota. Thus, even when there has been an element of specialism in the teaching, it has been difficult for tutors to develop their subject and to gain sustained feedback on the effect-iveness of their teaching. Some subjects have also been taught by tutors having little understanding of the nature of the generation of such know-ledge in that area or of current issues and debate. The outcome has been a static view of knowledge and research as separate from practice and from other knowledge, and a limited or negative view of specialisms in care, such as elderly care.

The subject specialism may be consistent with higher education – however, it creates a number of interesting challenges for nursing and midwifery! Few other disciplines bring together such a wide range of subjects, methodologies and related teaching approaches. For example, the assumed method in biological science is experimental. This positivist view of knowledge leads to the 'fact' itself being important learning together with discovery or observation for oneself, via the practical. Thus biological sciences tend to put a high priority on learning the material and on a high student–staff contact time. This is in sharp contrast to sociology where knowledge is seen as more problematic and bound up with issues of method, and where the emphasis in teaching is on debate, with the student being expected to both read extensively and reflect around a core of relevant topics. Teachers and students have to make sense of these widely different perspectives while the course as a whole must adjudicate between subject claims on timetabled and other student time. This debate will no doubt continue, particularly since students do experience conflicting demands on their time and attention, and the balance of workload remains uneven as the course is still at an early stage of implementation.

Participants in the course have also had to consider frameworks for knowledge in practice, particularly since such knowledge is equally dynamic and varied in nature. Practitioners in the health authority were using a variety of theoretical models for practice so although a systematic approach was assumed, it was not appropriate to select a specific model. Carper's (1978) taxonomy of knowledge in nursing offered a frame that was consistent with Benner's (1984) concept of expertise and with Schön's artistry (Schön, 1987). As discussed by Murphy and Reading in Chapter 3, initial statements of competence were drawn up, under Carper's headings of empirical, moral, personal and aesthetic (skill) knowledge. Subject inputs are largely included in empirical knowledge. The recognition and understanding of value systems, rights, duties and responsibilities are identified as moral knowledge. Feelings are recognized under personal knowledge while the bringing together of all these, in a unique response in assessing, planning, implementing and evaluating care, is seen as aesthetic knowledge, which also includes skills and techniques of care giving, such as physical and technical care, interpersonal support, teaching and environmental management. The statements of competence are being used as guides for staff and students in developing learning contracts and are subject to ongoing revision by a working group comprising lecturer practitioners from all five degrees, with further input from lecturers and students.

Beliefs about student learning

It follows from the beliefs outlined in the previous section that the students are acknowledged as central to their own learning. This ensures that reflection on practice is real, experience is turned into learning (Boud *et al.*, 1985) and that students establish the habit of life-long learning required of professional practitioners (UKCC, 1990). Central to this approach is a balance of student–teacher contact which allows students time to read and reflect, a feature of higher education which is relatively new to many nurse and midwifery programmes. Building on this basic requirement, a number of other techniques are being used to emphasize students' responsibility for their own learning. Many of the subject areas are assessed by coursework rather than examination, enabling students to focus on an area of specific interest to them. In their early social policy work, for example, students select a health topic of interest to them and build up a dossier about this topic from a variety of sources, including the media. Self and peer assessment also feature as contributory elements to subject grading and involve students in justifying marks awarded.

Students (and staff) are encouraged to write reflective diaries as a tool to develop their reflection and analysis on their experiences. These diaries are private but are used by students as a resource to contribute to discussions about their experiences in practice. They are also felt to be prerequisite to the practice-based learning contracts which form the major component of the assessment of practice competence (Murphy and Reading, Chapter 3).

Conclusion

The programme thus marks a radical shift from previous patterns of nurse and midwifery training. However, such a shift cannot take place without considerable change, including staff development. The integrated course development strategy outlined earlier has been particularly significant. The School of Nursing and Midwifery staff have become confident in debating with their Polytechnic colleagues; Polytechnic staff have become more knowledgeable about nursing and midwifery issues. Such processes have been further enhanced by a formal staff development programme. In addition to staff development relevant to the lecturer practitioner role (see Champion, Chapter 4), there have been workshops for all staff on a variety of topics such as lecturing to large groups, personal tutoring, marking at degree level and reflective practice. Although these are still required from time to time, attention is now focused on detailed curriculum development, particularly in relation to practice and the assessment of practice competence, and on complex issues such as interdepartmental roles, relationships and responsibilities. The Educational Methods Unit of the Polytechnic has played a valuable role in such staff development and there has also been an accelerated programme of staff release and secondment to gain higher, and in some instances first, degrees and full teaching qualifications.

The final outcome of this new programme has yet to be seen, as the four-year course is only in its second year of running. All the work being done is new and developmental so that it is a constant challenge. Some problems are becoming clearer, for example the very different nature of the various subject inputs and their demands on student time. In addition, the emphasis on coursework has resulted in students being overassessed, and in high staff workloads in relation to assessment. The practice base of the course also demands very close liaison with Directors of Nursing and Midwifery. However such liaison is greater than it has ever been and has resulted in course ownership being very much shared. Nevertheless, the sheer numbers of lecturer practitioners and clinical areas involved, spread throughout the eight health authority units, create major communication challenges in addition to a real resource distribution jigsaw.

It is clear however that this is a very different way of organizing professional education. Students, professional practitioners and polytechnic lecturers are in a new partnership. Practice development – which was the starting point of the initiative – has been accelerated and the programme itself is contributing to practice and staff development. In a very real way, practice and education have become inseparable and uniquely mutually stimulating.

References

Bendall, E. (1975) *So, You Passed Nurse.* London: Royal College of Nursing.

Benner, P. (1984) *From Novice to Expert: Excellence and Power in Clinical Nursing Practice.* Menlo Park, California: Addison-Wesley.

Boud, D., Keogh, R. and Walker, D. (eds) (1985) *Reflection: Turning Experience into Learning.* London: Kogan Page.

Carper, B. (1978) 'Fundamental patterns of knowing in nursing'. *Advances in Nursing Science,* 1, 13–23.

Chapman, C. (1985) *Theory of Nursing: Practical Application.* London: Harper & Row.

Crow, J. (1980) *Effects of Preparation on Problem Solving.* London: Royal College of Nursing.

Department of Health and Social Services (1972) *Report on the Committee of Nursing.* London: HMSO.

Dickoff, J. and James, P. (1968) 'A theory of theories: a position paper'. *Nursing Research,* 17(3), 197–203.

English National Board for Nursing, Midwifery and Health Visiting (1989) *Project 2000: 'A New Preparation for Practice'.* Guidelines and criteria for course development and the formation of collaborative links between approved training institutions within the National Health Service and Centres of Higher Education. London: ENB.

Fretwell, J. (1982) *Ward Learning and Teaching: Sister and the Learning Environment.* London: Royal College of Nursing.

Hunt, J. (1979) *The Teaching and Practice of Surgical Dressings in Three Hospitals.* London: Royal College of Nursing.

Kratz, C. (ed.) (1979) *The Nursing Process.* London: Bailliere Tindall.

Melia, K. (1987) *Learning and Working – The Occupational Socialisation of Nurses.* London: Tavistock.

Ogier, M. (1982) *An Ideal Sister? A Study of the Leadership Style and Verbal Interactions of Ward Sisters with Nurse Learners in General Hospitals.* London: Royal College of Nursing.

Orton, H. (1981) *Ward Learning Climate.* London: Royal College of Nursing.

Owen, G. (1984) *The Development of Degree Courses in Nursing Education – in Historical and Professional Context.* Polytechnic of the South Bank, Occupational Paper No. 4.

Roper, N., Logan, W. and Tierney, A. (1980) *The Elements of Nursing.* Edinburgh: Churchill Livingstone.
Schön, D.A. (1983) *The Reflective Practitioner.* London: Temple Smith.
Schön, D.A. (1987) *Educating the Reflective Practitioner.* London: Jossey-Bass.
Smith, J. (1981) *Nursing Science in Nursing Practice.* London: Butterworths.
United Kingdom Central Council for Nurses, Midwives and Health Visitors (1985) *Project 2000: A New Preparation for Practice.* London: UKCC.
United Kingdom Central Council for Nurses, Midwives and Health Visitors (1990) *Post Registration Education and Practice Project Report.* London: UKCC.
World Health Organization (1985) *Targets for Health for All by the Year 2000.* Copenhagen: WHO Regional Office for Europe.

Designing a Housing Course for the 1990s

Glen McDougall

Introduction

For a number of years, housing has been a well-developed area of teaching and research within the Faculty of Environment at Oxford Polytechnic. The School of Planning offered the most comprehensive teaching in housing, particularly in terms of a specialist route through the graduate one-year Diploma in Planning, but housing teaching was also an important part of the graduate Diplomas in Architecture and Design and a feature of the undergraduate course in the Department of Estate Management. Research in a number of areas of housing was a feature of all departments within the Faculty.

In 1988, in the context of devising the Faculty's Academic Plan, the School of Planning not only decided that it should try to consolidate its existing housing teaching but also that it was an appropriate time to develop specific housing courses aimed at meeting the particular requirements of housing practice and the profession. This case study concentrates on outlining aspects of course design and structure for one of the courses developed, the professional Diploma in Housing, which is fully recognized by the Institute of Housing.

Rationale for the Diploma in Housing

Everyone involved in housing education and practice is acutely aware that the housing system and types and levels of housing services are undergoing rapid change. Changing patterns of provision and management have increased the variety of organizations involved and the range of practices within these organizations. The powers and functions of housing agencies and the relationship between the public, private and voluntary/cooperative sectors are being transformed and this is not only changing housing policy but also the management practices and processes of housing production. Within this context, the definition and role of housing professionals and their relationship to the consumer/client in the housing development and management process are also being redefined.

In this situation of rapid change it was decided that it was not sufficient to train people within the existing guidelines of the Institute of Housing which had been laid down within a predominantly local authority housing management system and structure. There was a need for education of a specific kind which would both equip students to be effective housing development and management workers within the current housing system and enable them to be responsive and effective in an environment of continuing change. It was thought that developing knowledge about the range and variety of practice in the UK, and acquiring management skills which were transferable between different housing sectors, would be particularly important. Furthermore, given the increasing diversity and complexity of the housing service, students should be encouraged to develop specialist knowledge and skills based on their interest and the research and practice expertise of staff within the Faculty of Environment.

But educating for this new housing practice does not just require the acquisition of a range of knowledge and skills to ensure an efficient and effective housing service. It also demands a particular style of education which will encourage active learning, the interaction of theory and practice and the technical and substantive aspects of housing. Housing is an inter-disciplinary field and it was felt that this had led to some other housing courses having the appearance of a collection of different subjects and skills which were not strongly directed towards the activity of housing management. It was therefore decided that the focus of all courses should be on the knowledge and skills required for *operational housing practice* and that the course should be constructed to ensure the integration of different types of expertise and to enable the student progressively to appreciate the complexity of the relationship between theory and practice and the substantive and technical aspects of housing.

Course structure

It was decided to structure the course into two parts. The first part, taken on a one-year full-time or two-year part-time basis, provides the *orientation programme* for the new entrant to the housing profession. It aims to:

1. establish a general theoretical base for the teaching programme in such a way as to incorporate the diverse background experience of the stu-

dents and provide them with a basis for understanding the nature of the
housing system;
2. provide a critical exposition of British housing experience and practice
   through the analysis of current practice and historical and comparative
   study;
3. begin to develop the capabilities of students to engage in a variety of
   types of housing practice and provide a foundation for more specialist
   study in the second part of the course.

The *second part of the course*, which involves attendance at the Polytechnic
for one day a week, focuses on operational practice. It continues the development of the student's practice capabilities through core housing studies
(in policy making and analysis, development and design and housing management studies) and specialist studies in a choice of option areas (e.g.
voluntary sector servicing, economics and management of the housing stock).
The placement (or placements) in a housing organization is a major and
integral part of the course. The placement aims to provide practical experience of work in housing and to assist the integration of academic/profes-
sional and theory/practice aspects of the course. For example, placement
students are required to complete a practice notebook which not only sets
the framework for the student's work in placements but also becomes a
personal diary used for recording, consolidating and evaluating the experience of operating within a specific organizational setting.

Integrative themes

In the light of the analysis of the needs of housing practice and education
and in order to encourage integration and cohesion in the course content,
a number of themes were developed for the course. The themes identified
were:

(a) *The reflective practitioner* – encouraging students critically to examine
    the relationship between theory and practice in their work experience
    and developing skills and attitudes which will enable them to monitor
    and control their progress and professional development. This theme
    underpins all the core housing units in the Diploma in Housing. The
    model of the reflective practitioner is also developed through the active
    teaching and learning strategies devised for the course which encour-
    age both students and staff to monitor their progress and development
    through the course.
(b) *Responding to change* – understanding the processes of change within the
    housing system and acquiring and applying skills in the management of
    change. Within this theme, particular attention is paid to the manage-
    ment implications of the expanding role of the private sector and the
    development of the cooperative and housing association sectors. The
    location of the School in an area where the private sector is particularly

active and the housing association movement strong has meant that the staff have been interested in exploring throughout the course the changing face of the public sector and the developing relationship between public and private sectors and local authorities and housing associations. This theme, whilst underpinning units in the Orientation programme, is developed particularly in the core housing and placement studies of the second part of the course. Each of these units explores both the current housing system and the future shape of the system through comparative studies and uses a variety of teaching, learning and assessment methods (e.g. gaming, evaluation exercises, case studies) to assist students in the acquisition and application of skills which will enable them to respond positively to change.

(c) *The needs and rights of clients and consumers* – encouraging choice and participation in housing development and management of clients and consumers of the housing system and understanding the implications of this for management styles and procedures in the different housing sectors. Within this theme, the issues of *equal opportunities*, in terms of race, gender, disability and age, is emphasized and all units address this issue wherever appropriate. The course team strongly believed that the issue of equal opportunities should be integral to the course as a whole and should not be isolated and possibly marginalized in the course structure. Therefore they sought to ensure that the syllabuses for all units demonstrated the way in which this theme ran throughout the course.

(d) *Skill development for effective management* – encouraging the acquisition and application of specific skills for housing management. In the future, housing professionals are more likely to move between the different housing sectors than has been the case in the past. This means that professional education will need to emphasize increasingly the development of transferable skills which in turn will enable individuals to practise in the different sectors of the housing system. Although some basic skills have been programmed separately (e.g. statistical analysis and presentation) the majority of skills are acquired and applied within appropriate theoretical and practical work. Thus, for example, the acquisition of certain general accountancy skills is done within the context of housing finance and interpersonal skills are developed and practised in the context of project work which is a feature of most of the courses. Table 2.2 demonstrates the sequence of skill development and practical/project emphasis throughout the compulsory units of the Diploma in Housing.

Modes of delivery

In developing the Diploma course, the course team were conscious of the need to produce a course which could meet the needs of a variety of different types of students and the changing requirements of housing

Table 2.2 Skill development in compulsory units in diploma in housing

Unit number and title	*Skill emphasis*
9400.1 Introduction to housing: housing in action	Analysis and evaluation techniques. Introduction to group work skills and communication skills.
9401.1 Historical and theoretical approaches to housing	Use of historical research methods, contemporary sources and case study materials.
9302.1 Social and economic analysis	Application of social science concepts and techniques to housing issues. Report writing.
9402.2 Institutional and legal studies. 1: The agency environment	Institutional analysis. Legal and political awareness.
9403.3 Institutional and legal studies. 2: Housing law	Application of legal framework and statutory control to housing management issues.
9404.2 The housing development process. 1: Planning and development	Methods of local policy making and implementation. Valuation and financial appraisal techniques and application to development issues.
9405.3 The housing development process. 2: Design and construction	Critical analysis of design and briefing process. Application of construction, maintenance and repair knowledge to management of housing stock.
9309.1 Applied statistics	Statistical methods and analysis and their application. Presentation and communication of findings.
9406.2 Introduction to housing management. 1: The management of housing services	Development of general management skills and application to housing organizations. Development of key skills in personnel, financial and organizational management.
9407.3 Introduction to housing management. 2: Information systems	Application of microcomputing and operational research skills to housing management tasks.
9408.2 Housing finance	Application of financial control and management techniques to housing finance.
9409.3 Housing policy and practice	Personnel and organizational skills for managing change. Negotiative skills. Networking.

Table 2.2 (*continued*)

Unit number and title	Skill emphasis
9420.1 Housing policy issues	Evaluation of comparative evidence. Gaming and simulation techniques. Local policy analysis and implementation.
9421.2 Housing development and design issues	Evaluation and appraisal of housing stock. Skills in managing housing stock and user participation in design process.
9422.3 Housing management practice	Further development and application of skills in managing housing stock and managing people. Evaluation of own management skills. Facilitating techniques.
9423 Practice notebook	Development of individual management skills and self-evaluation and monitoring techniques. Synoptic skill assessment.
9488 Individual project	Synoptic skill assessment.

practice. Through consultation with housing teachers and practitioners and market research it was discovered there was:

- A continuing national need for full-time initial professional education for recent graduates
- A local need for part-time professional training for unqualified practitioners working in local housing agencies in the public, private and voluntary sectors
- A local practitioner need for continuing professional development.

In order to facilitate these different client groups, it was decided to adopt the unit credit system which is a feature of all graduate courses within the School of Planning. This system was initially considered because it provided greater scope for the development of student-centred learning methods and enabled assessment to be related more closely to teaching and learning objectives than linear course structures. It was adopted for graduate teaching because it:

- offered the possibility of developing a variety of different teaching methods within the norms of staff contact and student effort
- facilitated effective planning of the teaching programme, particularly for part-time and occasional students using the course for continuing professional development purposes
- was compatible with undergraduate teaching in the School and would facilitate interchange with other areas of the Polytechnic through the Modular Course.

The adoption of the unit credit system enables students to take the course by full-time, part-time or discontinuous study and facilitates continuing professional development as individual units can be taken by local practitioners. The experience of the School of Planning has been that there are distinct advantages in mixing full-time and part-time students on professional courses. The relationship between theory and practice and the interaction of different types of knowledge and expertise in project and seminar work are enhanced by the variety of the student body. Furthermore, there is a tendency where part-time students are taught separately from other students for them to be isolated from the mainstream of a department's activities and the quality of their educational experience to be less than that of full-time students.

The common graduate unit credit system is also a resource-efficient system. For example, within the Diploma in Housing Orientation programme, there are some contextual studies (concerned with the social, economic, political and spatial processes shaping housing policy, development and management) in which their general aspects can be separated from their specific application to the housing system. In these areas, units are shared with Diploma in Urban Planning Orientation programme students.

Conclusion

Through the principles of course design, modes of delivery and course structure, we have tried to produce a course which can be responsive to the needs of housing practice, enable students to become effective and efficient housing and management workers in the 1990s and meet the requirements of a professional institute. The success of the course will be judged in terms of the usefulness of its actual products and the ability of the course to continue to respond to the changing needs of housing practice.

Designing the Practicum in Teacher Education

Georgina Glenny and Elizabeth Hickling

This case study explores some of the principles that govern the design of practicum. It focuses on decisions about the nature of the practical experiences given to students training to become teachers. In the second part, examples are given of the way in which these principles have influenced the design of initial training courses for primary education at Oxford Polytechnic.

Students enter teacher education courses with a wealth of knowledge and experience that constitutes a basis for their professional development. This is particularly true of the 40 per cent of students who are 'mature', many of whom have been successful in other areas of work and may have experienced the schooling system from the vantage point of a parent or a governor. They will bring a range of theories about learning, the nature of schooling and the dynamics between the teacher and learner. At the same time they will have anticipations of a number of challenges and anxieties accompanying the training process itself. We consider that the acknowledgement of students' experiences and perceptions of their own needs should be central to their professional training. As McNamara notes, reviewing the work of a number of commentators from a range of discipline bases, all '... reinforce the requirement to start from and recognise the actor's situation and experience' (McNamara, 1990, p. 155).

The question is how to create a bridge between lay and professional experience, knowledge and concerns. We see the teacher educator's role as being one of helping students to explore, define, develop and perhaps reconstruct these theories, translating them into action in order to meet the professional demands that will be made upon them as a teacher. This process involves four main elements. The first is to enable students to make explicit, and present for challenge, their own internal models. Secondly, through practical, first-hand experience students need to acknowledge current practice in schools. Thirdly, they must critically consider the theoretical basis upon which current models of good practice are based. Fourthly, they need to mediate the previous processes in such a way as to inform their action as a reflective teacher. The four elements, although presented here discretely, are interwoven, but have particular weight and focus at varying times. Each has implications for the practicum.

In relation to the first element, clarification of individually held anticipations, beliefs and models for action is a necessary prerequisite for anyone involved in working closely with others. They should be open to question. Students will inevitably bring their own meanings to the experiences presented by the training institution and thus a wealth and variety of experience for reflection. It is this richness and diversity, however, that poses problems for the teacher educator in selecting a focus on desired elements at any given time. What kind of focus and what kind of environment provides the most appropriate bridge? We argue that to draw out effectively students' implicit models of learning, they need experience of being in the pupil's place by looking at learning at their own level. There are a number of reasons for this. First, it gives them a common experience with a group of other students allowing discussion to focus on variables which will be common to the group, if differently experienced. Secondly, it allows tutors to manipulate these variables, such as group structure, resourcing or session timings, in specific ways, to draw out professional issues most effectively. Thirdly, it allows them to look at the nature of curriculum in relation to their own experience and personal styles. Fourthly, it provides them with the space free from the pressures of the teacher's role, to develop a common language for dialogue about teaching and learning relationships. This last seems to be particularly important later in the course for sharing the multifarious experiences of classroom life and to enter wider professional debates.

In exploring the second element (supporting students through practical first-hand experience to acknowledge current practice in schools), the difficulty for the teacher educator is the complexity of the real-world context for action. Teaching is essentially interactive and subject to complex laws of cause and effect. If we hit a billiard ball with a cue, the consequences are mathematically predictable and subject to linear causality. If we become skilled enough, success can be assured. In persuading another person to move towards a particular objective, however, we enter the world of circular causality, in that reaction will depend on a number of circumstances that occurred in the past which, even with meticulous research, would not be measurable. This circular causality occurs with every interaction in the complex patterning of relationships in the classroom. The student, in entering the classroom with particular intentions, is faced by a group of children with a multiplicity of needs, rights and concerns that may confound those intentions. Further, she or he has to mediate the agenda of the class teacher, school and training institution. At the same time, even on the longest teaching practice, students are placed in a working context for such a short time that they do not experience the confidence that comes from knowing the situation well. Thus for the student, the classroom context is even more complex than for the class teacher.

The context remains complex no matter how we try to isolate discrete elements to allow students to practise particular skills. Thus instead of attempting to make the context apparently simpler, we have to acknowledge the complexity and organize it. As teacher educators we try to support students by creating an optimum context in which they are required to act and develop skills. If in so doing we simplify the context, we may well just create a situation that does not adequately reflect the real demands.

The pedagogical implications of this are challenging. Consider the analogy of the jigsaw. Discrete pieces are turned this way and that to fit into the whole picture. Each piece remains fixed and determined in its contribution. Each has a relation to the specific pieces on its borders as well as to the composite whole. Teacher education can take this form. Specific elements are taken for consideration and analysis: for example voice projection, classroom control and curriculum planning. If we assume this model, how do we come to define each jigsaw piece? Which element do we forefront at any given time and does it matter? In our handling of a jigsaw we may determine on the crucially identifying factor and build around it. Where would you start in the picture of the professional concerns: with the head teacher, the National Curriculum, special needs, the governing body, etc.? It is equally erroneous to assume that the final picture remains fixed and immutable. Quite clearly this is not the case. Recent ongoing legislation has convinced even the most conservative of teachers that the expectations on teachers, and their part in the education of children, are fluid, subject to conflicting demands and increasing complexity. The macro issues of politics, social change and economic considerations are interwoven with those of the specific contexts of schools and their environments to create an infrastructure to be interpreted variously by the participants. We come back to the notion of circular causality.

Yet quite clearly the student is required to be skilful in a number of ways. If we teach skills as discrete elements to be applied in specific predicaments, we create teachers who are looking for particular situations, who define situations in terms of the solutions they have available and in the worst scenarios, distort the situations they find themselves in to employ these particular approaches. The acquisition of skills can alternatively be seen as additions to the bank of resources from which the teacher, cognisant of the complex interplay of factors at any given time, may select. The acquired skills are to be viewed as being of service to the teacher. To return to the analogy of the jigsaw, the shape of each skill is determined by the context rather than structuring the context. A balance is maintained between anticipation and response.

Central to the third element (critical consideration of the theoretical basis upon which the current models of good practice are based) is giving students a variety of contexts so that they can make the comparisons necessary to draw out their own questions about purposes and methods. By broadening the base of the practicum and giving students experience of the behaviour of both children and adults, in a range of contexts, we enable them to bring in to sharp relief the particularity of classroom life.

This raises the whole question of the nature of the relationship between theory and practice. It has been frequently argued that this is not a linear one (McNamara, ibid., p. 148). Teaching involves acting intelligently in practical situations to achieve specified goals. So, while it is desirable for students to have access to a broad range of theory, this in itself is not sufficient for good practice. Students also need to select from theory in order to best inform their actions at any given time. Often in the classroom academic theoretical questions like 'is it true?' get replaced by more pragmatic concerns such as 'does it work?'. But even 'does it work?' is a complicated question, for example 'for whom?', 'in achieving what?, at 'what price?'.

This selection process may be a function of dominant personal constructions about teaching determining choices, such as commitment to creating optimum conditions for learning for individual children or commitment to social order within groups. These can change over time, given qualitative experiences which act significantly to challenge the student's thinking. This complex and fascinating area goes beyond the scope of this case study. However, by taking a role in a range of contexts we can support students in focusing on the choices that they observe in others and themselves and develop their ability to recognize the background of classroom decision making. For this focus to take place, choices about the nature of the practicum need to lead course design in such a way that students are appropriately briefed before their experience and given subsequent time for evaluation with tutors who have been involved in the placements.

The fourth element (mediation of the previous processes in such a way as to inform students' action as effective teachers) is concerned with the ways in which we draw together students' experiences of the course as a whole. Again, the role of the practicum cannot be separated from the other elements of the course. Here we are concerned with those things that help students to be successful in their practice in the classroom. It is crucial that what they are required to do allows them to see themselves as acting effectively, since this becomes a basis on which they can feel confident enough to experiment and test out their practice. Decisions about the practicum must provide developmental pathways that give such support, helping students make the best sense of what they already know and to prioritize what they need to come to know, through providing a range of contexts within which to act. Examples of our approach to this on present initial training courses are given below. Communicating the purposes of the activities is also critical, as students need to see themselves as developing skills and understandings that will support them in anticipation of their future role. At each stage the matching of experience to the students' perception of need is an important objective.

Approaches at Oxford Polytechnic

This approach to teacher training puts the practicum at the centre of course design, assuming varying emphasis as students' knowledge and skills develop. Like most teacher educators, we have designed a range of practicum elements in our courses, including: serial and block school experiences; practical individual and group projects, centred for example, on curriculum planning or evaluation of school policies; and the development, in the institution, of 'model classroom' environments for practical work, including working with children. Recent innovative developments include projects designed to facilitate the experience of being in the pupil's place, learning at the student's own level, to provide, as discussed earlier, a bridge to draw out previous student knowledge and experience and opportunities to consider professional issues free from the immediate pressures of the teaching role. All these elements reflect not only the centrality of the practicum but the increasing need to ensure it is a structured and mediated experience (Zeichner, 1990) through which students can progressively take on the complexities of the teaching role.

At the beginning of our courses we provide what we hope will be a rich learning context to which we expect students to respond at their own level. In the undergraduate programme this involves several days' study of a local area whilst in the post-graduate programme the starting point for enquiry is a local museum. Students are involved in both individual study and in group work, leading to a collective presentation of their enquiries. Simultaneously they have access to workshops on relevant skills together with process seminars to share and analyse their experiences. They are encouraged to make explicit, and offer for peer examination, immediate issues concerning their own learning such as a tendency to start with historical rather than scientific questions, or to express ideas through words or music rather than dance or drama. They can experience the frustration of interruptions to their work generated by somebody else's timetable and the pleasures and problems of working in different kinds of groups. Further, they can witness their own response to the learning situation, identify the nature and quality of the learning experienced and assess the factors that contributed to or detracted from it. In so doing they will be raising the important questions which will form a framework for looking in classrooms and will be initiated into the professional debates concerning areas such as curriculum and pedagogy.

Much has already been said about the complexity of the classroom and the need to select the focus for activities, which may be achieved in a number of ways. Our initial approach has been to focus the complexity by setting up specific activities drawing from students' experiences at their own level as described above. These might include comparing children's learning with adult learning and examining the effect of context on children's behaviour. As well as looking at a range of school contexts, such observation work for students may be extended by looking at children's learning and behaviour in the wider community, for example, in play parks or the local swimming pool. The curriculum focus can be achieved by requiring students to develop a contained project involving the whole planning cycle that can be carried out through ongoing classroom activities, for example, working with a group of children to set up a stimulus display for the rest of the class (for details of this methodology, see Russell and Watt, 1990). Such activities can facilitate a debate concerning the interface between the developing understanding of children's individual needs and the requirements of a given curriculum. At the same time they enable students to directly address issues of planning, organization, management and evaluation and to practise practical skills recently learned. Again, briefings for these activities will include skills-based workshops and follow-up feedback sessions.

An important feature of initial work in school is ensuring success for the student. The design of course elements which parallel particular skills developed at the student's own level and the activities engaged in with children is one way of achieving this. Another is the use of modelling by staff of activities which can be replicated by the student and which are likely to be successful in producing quality work. This maximizes the possibility that students are able to reflect on positive experiences of themselves in role. The central training experience for the student will be the taking on of the teacher role, and the organization of the practicum, particularly in block school placements, must aim to confirm the student in this experience. The tutor works closely with the students, supporting and monitoring the planning process for classroom activities, giving feedback about what they are achieving and identifying appropriate points for development.

The classroom-based perspective can be extended by placements that focus on the whole school, either explicitly by examination of whole school policies or through projects where a group of students and their tutor are involved in a school-wide problem-solving activity, for example, developing a school's environmental areas. In the wider context, placements are arranged that ensure students have a chance to be aware of, and respond to, other groups concerned with the schooling process. This might include sessions with parents' groups, placements in special forms of provision or shadowing people in specific roles, such as advisers or educational psychologists. We have also experimented with training alongside other professional groups, for example, working with social work students on themes of child abuse.

Placing the practicum at the centre of course design requires effective communication with schools so that a range of school settings and activities can be provided. Clearly, this is not a reasonable expectation without a close relationship with schools which ensures a joint commitment to the project through a sense of reciprocity and mutual respect for each other's contributions and concerns. In practice this requires good personal relationship to be established between the school experience tutors and particular groups of schools, in a context where organizational principles are clear to all concerned. One of the ways of sharing our anticipations of what we expect from students has been through joint work with schools in production of a profile to monitor progression and development of student learning. Such joint work has been of limited extent but of great value and we hope to develop this further. As well as ensuring a sharing of agenda amongst those involved in providing the training experience, it makes explicit to students how their training can enable them to achieve. Students then have ways of explicitly acknowledging what they bring to the course, supporting them in shaping their own learning experiences to their particular needs.

Initial training is only the beginning of a student's professional development. We seek to establish a patterning that can become a style for further professional approaches, based on a clear cycle of action, experience, analysis and reflection, which includes preparation for examination by significant others. We hope that this will stand students in good stead to meet the challenges in the changing world of education, as confident, articulate professionals.

References

McNamara, D. (1990) 'Research on teacher thinking: its contribution to educating student teachers to think critically'. *Journal of Education for Teaching*, **16**(2), 147–60.

Russell, T. and Watt, D. (1990) *Science Processes and Concept Exploration Project – Research Reports – Growth*. Liverpool: Liverpool University Press.
Zeichner, K. (1990) 'Changing directions in the practicum: looking ahead to the 1990s'. *Journal of Education for Teaching*, **16**(2), 105–32.

Course Design for Professional Accreditation

Denise Morrey

The School of Engineering at Oxford Polytechnic runs a CNAA validated BEng(Hons) in Engineering. During the 1989–90 academic session the course was scheduled for a major quinquennial review. The members of staff who had been closely involved with the course saw this as an ideal opportunity to take a fresh look at the structure, direction and purpose of both its content and approach. This case study describes the rationale behind the design process and the structure used; it also seeks to illustrate how the various inputs from external sources were drawn together in order to create a package which would ultimately satisfy what can often be quite diverse or even conflicting requirements.

The BEng(Hons) in engineering

The BEng(Hons) in engineering is a three-year full-time or four-year sandwich programme which allows students to specialize in either mechanical or electronics engineering. There is a common first year studied by all students and at the end of this they choose their specialism. During the second and third years there is a common core of subjects which all students study along with material specific to their chosen discipline. The course has been developed with Design as an integrating feature, allowing students from the two specialist areas to work together on real engineering problems and to use their specialist knowledge in the solution of these problems.

A major revision of the course

In redesigning the course, the Course Planning Committee took a top–down approach, taking as a starting point the aims of the course from the point of view of prospective students, employers of graduates, and the professional engineering institutions (Institution of Mechanical Engineers and Institution of Electrical Engineers).

However, building on our experiences of running the course since 1974 and in an attempt to respond and carry out modifications in line with comments from external examiners, accreditation visits from the IMechE and IEE, and feedback from students, it was felt that there were also a number of major issues which the redesign should address the following:

(i)   The class contact hours and workload in the existing course were high when compared with other courses in engineering and technology, and students have to study most subjects in parallel throughout the three terms, with examinations taking place at Easter and the end of the summer term. A reduction in the number of contact hours and the adoption of a unit-based structure where subjects are studied and examined over one term, with a study week in week 10, was proposed. This also offered the benefits that the course could be easily updated, allowing the School to respond more quickly to both internal and external pressure for change, and it would facilitate the timetabling of the course, allowing slotting with the Polytechnic Modular Course.

It was recognized that this change would require a somewhat different approach to teaching and learning by both staff and students; there would be less time to assimilate knowledge than before.

(ii)   It was felt that there needed to be more integration across subject boundaries, particularly into the area of Design, since this is seen as being the central core of the course. It was also felt that this would aid the students in their transfer of knowledge between disciplines. It was therefore decided to devote the majority of the third term to project and experimental-based activities, which most staff would be involved in teaching.

(iii) The industrial environment in which most professional engineers now practise has strong implications for the type of education which they require. The pace of technological change throughout manufacturing industry means that graduates need to be involved in a programme of continuing education during the rest of their working lives. It is important that they acquire study skills and the tools of independent learners. In addition, many engineers work in a multidisciplinary environment, and as they take on responsibility become more involved in the managerial and business functions of the industry in which they work. It was therefore essential that a new course addressed these needs.

(iv)   Demographic changes in the next five years will result in a fall in the number of school-leavers available to enter higher education; there has been a drop in the number of A level students studying physics at school; and it is still recognized that engineering is unpopular as both a course choice and a career when compared with many of the other professions. Along with the sharp changes in both marketing and admissions practices which have been adopted by the School, it was felt that much could be done to the structure of the course in order to make it more attractive to prospective students. This was identified as an important means of maintaining entry standards and student numbers. A particularly important point was the provision of a wider choice of options in the final year of the course.

(v) In the past many of our students (not unlike engineering students in other institutions) have seemed to be badly motivated, and it has been noticed that students often have difficulty in transferring knowledge and skills from one part of the course to another, particularly in the area of design where it is necessary for them to apply their under-standing to more open-ended tasks. In response to this it was felt that a more flexible structure which enabled staff to use alternative ap-proaches to teaching and learning, and in particular more project-based and student-centred activity was desirable. It was felt that by allowing students to take a more active part in their learning that this would improve their motivation and the level of understanding achieved. It was also acknowledged that many more children being educated under the GCSE system would be used to a flexible ap-proach to teaching which more closely mirrored the world of industry and commerce which we were preparing them for.

(vi) There had been a great deal of interest expressed by local companies in the idea of providing one-year industrial placements for our stu-dents on a thick sandwich basis. This has largely arisen as a result of the success of the industrial field course.

(vii) The advent of the European Market in 1992 prompted the need for more awareness of European lifestyle and the teaching of a Euro-pean language for those who had already attained a basic level of competency.

Despite the areas of change which were identified, it was felt that there were many aspects of the existing course which worked well and should be retained, in particular, the common core of material studies by both mech-anical and electronics engineering students in the second and third years, and the integration between disciplines through group design projects. The coverage of fundamental principles in the first year of the course, followed by applications, was seen as being a sound, logical approach.

In arriving at the final structure for the course in terms of subject mix, balance of lecture, seminar and practical time, and the pattern of assess-ments used, a great deal of background reading and investigation was done and there was wide debate amongst the staff involved. The following sources were used:

(i) Information produced by those involved in the current debate on engineering education, such as the Engineering Council (1988), the Engineering Institutions (Engineering Council, 1984 and IMechE,

1988) and their Accreditation Panels (IMechE, 1988), the CNAA Committee for Engineering (1988), and the Design Council (1985).

(ii) Criticisms and observations made by External Examiners to the course and visiting parties such as IMechE and IEE Accreditation Panels and CNAA Validation Panels.

(iii) Information about the needs of industry offered from industrial advisers and the School's industrial contacts.

(iv) The debate within higher education as a whole regrading the provision of Education for Enterprise, training in transferable skills, and the widening of access to courses.

(v) Information on the possible application of alternative teaching, learning and assessment methods provided by consultation with the Educational Methods Unit in the Polytechnic, and by access to publications in this area (Cowan, 1986).

(vi) Debate within the School and Course Planning Committee about the possible direction and structure of a new course.

In addition, draft proposals for the structure were circulated to external advisers from other academic institutions and local industry for comments and feedback, and considered by student representatives at a series of meetings.

Because of the nature of engineering degree courses as a professional qualification, it is important to consider the role and influence of the engineering institutions in the process of course design. In order for an engineer to practise in this country it is not mandatory that he or she is registered as a Chartered Engineer. Similarly engineering degree courses do not need to be accredited by the professional institutions (accreditation exempts students from the academic requirements for membership of the institutions and chartered status). However, well-informed eighteen-year-olds and others wanting to study for an engineering qualification realize the benefits of chartered status, particularly for those wanting to change jobs to work abroad, and that accreditation of a course is a good sign of quality. In these difficult times of recruitment such considerations are of paramount importance and cannot be ignored.

Whilst it is easy to follow some of the guidelines laid down by the institutions, satisfying a number of masters can be a difficult juggling act. The BEng course has a substantial amount of common material which both mechanical and electronics students study. However the recommendations laid down by the two learned bodies responsible for accreditation differ quite considerably; the IMechE favours a significant amount of time being devoted to management, communication and business studies (as did all of our external advisers); the IEE is unhappy to see what it regards as the watering down of the analytical content and depth by the inclusion of this material; students favoured the inclusion of a foreign language, but staff were nervous about the reduction of contact hours claiming that it would no longer be possible to 'cover' the material required in order to educate students to a level which would satisfy the engineering institutions.

The course was successfully validated with only minor modifications and has been running in its present form since September 1990. Both staff and students have not found the transition to the termly-based unit structure easy, but the students favour this approach since it helps them to manage their time and concentrate their efforts, and it has given staff a much better feel for what material really needs to be covered and the other pressures which the students face.

The course has recently been visited by the IMechE for reaccreditation (June 1990). As ever they were thorough and rigorous in their assessment and analysis of the course. They welcomed the coherent thread of management and communication studies in all three years, but they urged further reduction of student contact hours in line with what is happening at other institutions. The discussion which we had was both frank and helpful, and their comments reassuring. They also welcomed the possibility of a joint accreditation visit with the Institution of Electrical Engineers.

Satisfying a number of different professional bodies and providing what both staff, students and employers feel is a professional education is often a matter of compromise between the different interests. It is also necessary to realize that major changes are not always possible in a short space of time given the limited resources which we have to work with and the existing culture of higher education. We feel that the structure which we have produced provides a more attractive and flexible base for developments in the next five years, largely because of our approach to the course design. Without such a major review which tried to take in all the issues currently being addressed and discussed in the field of engineering education, this would not have been possible.

References

CNAA Committee for Engineers (1988) *CNAA Conference on Recent Developments and Future Prospects for Engineering Degree Courses, Solihull, June 1988*. London: CNAA.

Cowan, J. (1986) 'Challenges in teaching and assessment – Eight awkward questions about engineering curriculum today'. *EPC/CEP Conference on Learning and Assessment Methods in Engineering Education, September 1986*.

Design Council (1985) *Curriculum for Design – Engineering Undergraduate Courses. Sharing Experience in Engineering Design (SEED)*. London: Design Council.

Engineering Council (1984) *Standards and Routes to Registration (SARTOR)*. London: Engineering Council.

Engineering Council (1988) *An Integrated Engineering Degree Programme*. Consultative Document. London: Engineering Council.

Institution of Mechanical Engineers (1985) *The Formation of Mechanical Engineers* (The Grant Report). London: Institution of Mechanical Engineers.

Institution of Mechanical Engineers (1988) *Accreditation in Practice*. Seminar, April 1988.

Accreditation of Company Training Programmes

Clive Robertson

The development of a currency, the 'credit', to describe the quality and quantity of academic achievement in Credit Accumulation and Transfer Schemes (CNAA, 1990) enables evaluation and comparison of learning outcomes achieved in a range of learning environments – not least of these the very real opportunities of personal development and learning offered in company training programmes (Continuing Education Standing Committee, 1988).

Accreditation of company training programmes offers a range of benefits to the individual and to the company, as well as to academics and academic institutions. First, ownership of learning and training goals by the individual, and reward for achievement as credit which can be accumulated towards a recognized qualification, can be a powerful motivation and incentive for high standards of performance. This in turn enriches the company's performance and the training programmes which it offers. The company and the training programme also benefit from the need to define expected outcomes of training and performance criteria, to develop systems for assessment, feedback and quality monitoring, and to establish an appropriate culture which supports individual development and recognizes the links between individual performance and training and development needs.

An accredited programme can offer a competitive edge in the recruitment market as employers jostle to attract and retain staff (*Wall Street Journal*, 1987). Long-term prospects for company-linked training which also offers personal rewards in terms of nationally recognized qualifications is an attractive benefit for companies to offer and can reduce staff turnover if accredited training is progressive and leads to high levels of achievement and thus higher qualifications (Robertson and Glendining, 1989; Wallis and Currell, 1989).

The academics involved in accreditation exercises gain opportunities for close partnerships with employers and employees, first-hand contact with current business and commercial developments as well as human resource development methods. Reciprocally, the company gains access to the resources of the academic institute, to wider contextual views of its particular business area and its human resource development methods, and opportunities to develop and upgrade the quality of its training. Long-term articulation between company-based training and programmes from the current prospectus of the academic institute is facilitated. Two case histories from Oxford Polytechnic serve to identify the key features of accreditation of company training programmes.

Company A

This is a large multinational fast-food company recruiting a wide range of individuals to different functional levels in its organization. Training and development in-company enables promotion to restaurant management level and above for individuals with no formal prior qualifications or experience although the company also recruits graduates and those with equivalent qualifications. Training programmes offered by the company were examined by academics from Oxford Polytechnic at the request of the Management Development Manager, based in the company's training department. The programme offered at the Assistant Restaurant Management development level was thought to be capable of achieving outcomes broadly equivalent to those achieved by first-year undergraduates on a Hotel and Catering Management degree course. Individuals who completed this programme would move to Restaurant Management. The programme consisted of some 40 individual work-based projects which encouraged experiential learning and which were completed over the period of 9–18 months depending on the background of the individual manager.

Proposals were made on the company's behalf to CNAA that successful completion of the programme could, with the development of suitable assessment strategies, be equivalent to 120 credits at level I of an undergraduate programme (CNAA, 1990). Furthermore, selected projects from the programme could be undertaken at levels 2, 3 and M depending on the previous qualifications and experience of individuals. The CNAA accepted these proposals subject to academic assessment and monitoring procedures being developed and the appointment of external examiners by the CNAA.

Having made such exciting progress (this was the first direct application to CNAA by a company), meeting the assessment requirements now became problematic. Accreditation had been undertaken at the instigation of the training department of the company and there was no broad recognition within the company of its value. Conflicting rumours abounded about what had been achieved. 'Operations' staff to directorate level were not convinced of the merits of accreditation or its relevance to the company's needs. The investment necessary to develop appropriate assessment, feedback and quality monitoring systems was not forthcoming. A small-scale pilot exercise involving some eight trainees with their regional managers acting as tutors made limited progress. Finally, the company was subject to a takeover involving major changes of personnel and implementation of a new and quite different approach to management development.

Unit B

This is a unit providing training for non-medical staff within the National Health Service. Its Junior Management Development programme is designed for graduates or Higher National Diplomates, and, more commonly, individuals who have been promoted from supervisory positions. The programme is designed as a series of modules which involve residential and work-based components. Experiential learning is encouraged through cycles of active participation and reflection. Assessment and feedback is well developed with the roles of mentors and tutors clearly established.

Academics from the Polytechnic were asked to make a thorough evaluation of the programme and to make recommendations to the CNAA on credit rating. Time was spent at the residential stages of the programme observing training activities, talking with tutors, tutees and programme directors; trainees were visited at the workplace, and the programme was discussed with those involved in supporting trainees at the workplace. The backgrounds and qualifications of those recruited to the programme were examined and the junior management roles which they would play after the programme. Comparison of learning outcomes achieved were made with those achieved in equivalent undergraduate programmes. A yardstick used in early comparisons was the hours of student effort required to complete the programme versus those of an undergraduate student.

Several months were spent on this phase in the accreditation process and during this time improvements to the programme, the supporting documentation and assessment strategies were discussed with the unit staff and implemented by them. Development needs of tutors involved in assessment were considered and plans implemented.

Finally, a proposal was prepared for the CNAA, recommending that the programme should have a credit rating of 120 level 2 credits. This was agreed by the CNAA and the programme is now under way with an academic from Oxford Polytechnic acting as external examiner and reporting to the CNAA, while other academics are members of the programme's management committee. Development of internal confidence and experience in assessment is recognized as critical and being worked on. The programme looks forward to a successful accredited future.

These two contrasting examples were to point up a number of key factors in accreditation (Robertson, 1990).

(i)   There must be awareness throughout the company or organization of accreditation and its potential benefits. Accreditation must be embedded in the human resource development culture. It requires recognition and encouragement if it is to be successful from all sectors and levels in the company and organization. In company A the accreditation of the programme was not internally marketed, not understood by those outside the training area and may, indeed, have been threatening to them as enhanced skills of coaching, counselling and assessment would require development. In unit B, accreditation of the programme was recognized as a natural development step. There was an organizational culture within the NHS to support such a development.

(ii) Academics must be prepared to invest considerable time and energy in becoming familiar with the programme to be accredited. An open and frank dialogue between company personnel and academics is essential. There must be room for movement on both sides, with the company recognizing the need to demonstrate learning outcomes and make assessment of them if credit is to be awarded, and preparedness on the part of academics to accept novel forms of assessment, not to require the construction of assessment 'hurdles' which are irrelevant to the company's needs, and to 'demystify' the assessment procedure. The 'gap' between industry and the academe is often one of language or jargon. We are often saying the same things but using different words!

(iii) Judgements on credit value require a number of inputs and decisions should not be reached until they have been sufficiently explored. These include:

- the qualification or quantifiable experience of recruits
- the nature of positions which individuals will hold or may aspire to on completion of the programme
- the aims and objectives of the programme, performance criteria, and methods of assessment
- comparison of programme outcomes with those achieved in taught undergraduate and postgraduate courses
- evaluation of the programme in terms of requirements for undergraduate and post-graduate courses described in the CNAA handbook
- assignment of levels and numbers of credits using CNAA guidelines
- the methods used to encourage learning and development
- links between individual expectations and needs and the opportunities provided by the programme
- monitoring, coaching, counselling, appraisal and assessment skills available within the company
- the level of commitment required of the student in terms of study hours and comparison with undergraduate and post-graduate programmes
- the methods of ensuring transfer of learning to the workplace
- clear agreement by the company to make improvements, if appropriate, in programme design, delivery and assessment
- clear agreement by the company to invest in long-term staff development for those staff involved in programme design, delivery and assessment
- clear agreement by the company to engage in a long-term partnership with academics to ensure the maintenance of academic standards.

References

CNAA (1990) *Handbook 1990–91*. London: CNAA, pp. 195–201.

Continuing Education Standing Committee (1988) *A Strategy for the Future of Vocational Continuing Education*. London: National Advisory Body.

Robertson, C. (1990) 'Giving credit where it's due'. In Leslie, D. and Watson, S. (eds) *Hospitality Management – Current Issues and Future Development*. Najui Polytechnic.

Robertson, C. and Glendining, G. (1989) 'Accreditation of company management development programmes in the hospitality industry'. *International Journal of Hospitality Management*, **8**(3), 191–6.

Wallis, S.E. and Currell, B.R. (1989) 'Accreditation of in-company training – approaches and opportunities'. *Training and Development*, June 1989.

Wall Street Journal (1987) 'Companies' education investment pays dividends', 26 October.

3

Course Delivery and Assessment

Hazel Bines

In Chapter 2, two main models of professional education within higher education were identified, namely the technocratic and the post-technocratic models. Each of these has implications for the delivery and assessment of courses, but common issues include the following: the choice of the most effective methods of teaching, learning and assessment; developing the learning environment; and the integration of the student's experience of different course elements, such as contributory academic disciplines, the concepts and theories of professional knowledge and action and the practicum. For the post-technocratic model, further issues include the following: the contextualization of academic disciplines within the study of professional knowledge and action; the development of the practicum as a structured experience; and ensuring that professional competence remains the central and integrating focus of the course.

Paradoxically, although professional courses are primarily concerned with the development of effective practice, there has not until recently been an extensive debate about the practices of teaching and learning in education for the professions. The major concerns in the development, validation, accreditation and delivery of courses have been the content and range of the professional knowledge base and the role and effectiveness of practical placements and experience in developing professional competence. Although professional courses may draw on a wide range of teaching, learning and assessment methods, there has been little research on which of these are most suitable and effective. The now substantial literature on adult learning has not been applied to education for the professions in a systematic way and, with the exception of some useful and important publications, debate has largely centred on developing effective teaching and learning for discrete professions, rather than the practice of professional education as a whole.

It is beyond the scope of this book to consider in depth the major issues involved in teaching, learning and assessment in professional courses. However we can identify an agenda for future debate, research and practice, with particular reference to the development of the post-technocratic model and the institutional and other contexts within which it may be implemented. This includes the impact on teaching and learning methods of trends in professional education such as new partnerships between employers and educators, the development of employment-based learning, the growing importance of continuing professional development, the increasing expectations of both students and their varied sponsors and the exigencies of funding and resources. Before these are discussed in more detail, some general consideration will be given to models and methods of teaching and learning in professional education.[1]

Teaching and learning in professional education

As noted above, a number of questions surround the teaching of academic disciplines, professional theory, practical skills, problem-solving and a reflective approach to practice. It is also important, drawing on a key axiom of most of the current literature on adult learning, to frame such questions in terms of the learning experiences of students, with teaching methods being seen as a corollary of, rather than antecedent to, such debate. In addition, professional education, with its emphasis on developing action as well as knowledge, makes particularly difficult demands on educators. Nevertheless there are some principles and models to act as starting points and a number of approaches and techniques which have been used successfully to date.

Although the types of approach to higher and other adult education suggested by a number of authors have not been systematically applied to education for the professions, their use is certainly characteristic of many, though not all, professional courses, and they have formed the basis of most recent literature on such education, as a suggested model of 'good practice'. They are based, in part, on the seminal differentiation by Knowles (1978) of 'pedagogy' and 'andragogy'. This differentiation is somewhat problematic because of the gender implications of the term 'andragogy' and the lack of recognition given to the long-standing traditions child-centred and experiential, as well as transmission-based, approaches to the teaching of children. Nevertheless it has contributed to the identification of some important principles pertinent to professional education. These include the following: the recognition of the learner as increasingly self-reliant and autonomous; task or problem-centred rather than subject-based learning; using the learner's experience as a resource; partnership between teacher and learner in relation to the diagnosis of learning needs and the curriculum; the use of experiential and enquiry-based methods of learning; and a criterion-referenced approach to assessment. Such principles have since been used to develop a range of approaches to adult learning, both for professional education and for higher education as a whole (e.g. Rowntree, 1981; Jarvis,

1983; Goodlad, 1984; Boud, 1985, 1988; Rogers, 1986; Gibbs, 1987; Brown and Atkins, 1988).

A particularly significant characteristic of such approaches to adult learning and higher education is their close correlation to the concerns and practices of professionalism and professional education, including, for example, the importance of self-reliance, autonomy and problem-solving in the professional role and the focus in education on enquiry, experience and competence. These approaches could thus be seen as providing a 'tailor-made' methodology of education for the professions, although they were not developed for this explicit purpose. Consequently, rather than having to develop a new or different approach, the key task is to link, and then develop and refine, an extant and extremely useful body of theory and practice. Apart from the obvious benefits in terms of saving both labour and time, this has the added advantage of placing education for the professions squarely within the debate on the development of teaching and learning in higher education as a whole.

Future developmental work should therefore focus on two main issues. First, identifying and remedying areas of mismatch between 'good practice' in adult/higher education and the approaches of professional courses and secondly, refining and extending such approaches, both for specific professions and professional education as a whole. Leaving aside the degree to which practice within particular courses, professions and institutions has embraced more innovative approaches to teaching and learning, there are several key areas of continuing mismatch with 'good practice' as outlined above. For example, although professional courses have tried to adopt practical, experiential and problem-based methods for the professional theory and practice elements of courses, the same approach has not always been used in the teaching of contributory academic disciplines. Equally, not enough has been done to ensure that teachers and learners jointly identify and negotiate learning needs and curriculum. Thirdly, although continuous professional development (CPD) courses generally acknowledge student autonomy and maturity, this is not always true of initial courses, particularly where they are largely taken by younger adult learners.

In turn, there are a number of key issues relevant to the further development and refining of methods. For example, much still needs to be done to find or improve solutions to special, and often complex questions, such as how to develop effective experiential learning, problem-based learning and interdisciplinary study. There is also the requirement to develop methods appropriate to the new modes of delivery discussed in Chapter 2, such as part-time, open and employment-based learning. Due to the complexity of professional action, the issue of progression is a further important aspect of such discussion, and much also needs to be done to develop effective and supportive approaches to assessment, in particular the assessment of professional competence in the practicum. Some of these questions are now considered in more detail.

Developing the practice of professional education

Academic disciplines

As noted in Chapter 2, professional education has traditionally been based on a combination of contributory pure and applied disciplines and professional theory and practice. The knowledge base provided by the disciplines may include both epistemological, methodological and empirical elements of the discipline in its 'pure' form and a selection of substantive issues and applications considered to be most relevant to the profession in question. Thus the teaching of sociology, for example, may include elements of sociological theory and methods, coupled with industrial sociology for managers and engineers, urbanization for planners and the sociology of the family for social workers. Similarly, although all health care professionals will encounter some of the general methodological and empirical aspects of the life sciences, a selection of particular topics will be made on the grounds of both relevance and required level of understanding.

However, there is increasing dissatisfaction with such approaches, arising from general critique of the technocratic model (as discussed in Chapter 2) and from the realization that they may not be particularly effective in developing the knowledge and understanding required. Moreover, such concern is evident in relation to a number of professions and disciplines, ranging from the questioning of the suitability of the medical model of life science teaching for nursing (Akinsanya, 1987) to recognition of student hostility and indifference to sociology in engineering courses (Glover and Kelly, 1987). In addition, due to increasing confidence in the value and rigour of professional education *per se* and the new emphasis on competence, the credibility of courses is no longer seen to rest on the amount and level of 'academic' study or 'personal' academic development of the student, but rather on the effectiveness and relevance of learning for professional requirements. As noted in Chapter 2, contributory academic disciplines are thus increasingly being contextualized in professional theory, issues and practice.

This contextualized approach has two main elements. Firstly it continues the tradition of selecting relevant substantive, applied topics or issues from the discipline in question. However, such topics are taught with specific reference to pertinent professional concerns; the knowledge of the discipline being used to inform, critically examine and analyse the nature of (and solution to) that concern. Secondly, the methodological approaches of the discipline may be used to develop the capacity for enquiry and research into profession-related phenomena and practice. For example, both life and behavioural science enquiry methods may be taught to nurses, to develop their capacity to observe physiological and psychological reactions to illness and health care intervention (Akinsanya, op. cit.; Wattley and Muller, 1987). In addition the social sciences may be further used to examine the profession itself, including professional beliefs, action and organization (see Astley, below; Glover and Kelly, op. cit.).

However, although this approach is more congruent with the conceptions of professional action and education intrinsic to the post-technocratic model, it raises some new difficulties. The structures of knowledge, methods of enquiry and empirical knowledge and phenomena relevant to the profession may well not match those of the discipline(s) involved. The profession-based framing of teaching and learning, together with the sheer volume of what is considered necessary to learn, may thus distort and undermine the nature of the discipline, leading, for example, to the teaching of substantive topics without reference to formal theory, or the uncritical use of enquiry methods which are still being debated within the discipline itself. Similarly, the trend towards integrating a number of disciplines relevant to particular professional topics raises a range of academic and organizational difficulties in relation to developing interdisciplinary work (which will be further discussed in Chapter 5). There is also the question of effective teaching and learning methods, particularly since some of the traditional methods of teaching and assessing the academic disciplines, such as lectures, seminars, library or laboratory-based work, essays and examinations are unlikely to facilitate integrated, topic- or problem-based professional learning. Effective learning methods are also very important to the general development of professional courses and will now be briefly discussed.

Effective learning

Teaching and learning methods for professional education, particularly the post-technocratic model, are particularly concerned with three main aspects of professional development, namely the professional knowledge base, competence in professional action and the development of reflection. As noted in Chapter 2 and above, the interrelationship of these three elements, and the growing emphasis on competence, are increasingly leading to an integrated topic or theme-based curriculum, allied to a range of structured practica, within which students progressively experience and reflect on the complexities of the professional role. The most appropriate methods of teaching and learning would thus seem to be those which are concerned with enquiry, analysis, experience and problem-solving. This paradigm of 'good practice' is further sustained by the new approaches to adult/higher education discussed earlier and the similarities between the experiential learning cycle (Kolb, 1984), problem-solving and the cycle of reflective professional practice. There is thus now considerable interest in experiential, and particularly, problem-based approaches to teaching and learning. As well as modelling the 'swampy lowland' actualities of unique, often value-laden problems of professional action (Schön, 1987), such learning techniques can integrate knowledge and action, structure progression through increasingly complex problems and encourage independent study and life-long learning (Neufeld and Chong, 1984; Boud, 1985; Cawley,

1989). Problem-based learning (PBL) also facilitates student autonomy and negotiation of the curriculum and, when allied to small group work, is not only more effective but includes communication and other interpersonal and collaborative skills which have often been neglected in professional education despite being crucial to successful professional action (Boud, op. cit.; Cawley, op. cit.; Jaques, 1984).

PBL also seems to offer solutions to one of the major issues in course design and delivery, discussed earlier and in Chapter 2, namely the development, centrality and integration of the practicum. It provides a rationale and method for designing and delivering a course primarily as a practicum whilst maintaining opportunities for students to focus on particular issues, without having to attend to all the complexities of a full professional role or setting. Experiences of institution-based practica, using PBL, can then be further elaborated in the workplace, particularly if this practicum is also carefully structured and mediated (cf. Glenny and Hickling, Chapter 2).

However, much still needs to be done to develop techniques of PBL,[2] together with other methods of learning, whether in higher education institutions or professional work settings, including the role and effectiveness of learning techniques such as participant observation, modelling, routine practice, conscious experimentation and collaborative teamwork with an experienced professional. As discussed by Astley and Hayward below, the use of research and other enquiry techniques, drawn from the natural and social sciences, together with methodologies such as the design process in engineering or architecture, is also an important element of professional education, in both initial and CPD courses. For CPD courses in particular, as Lewis has noted in relation to teacher education, the use of action research in the student's own professional setting will not only develop enquiry and management skills but also has the potential to integrate the practicum, that is the student's professional role, within the course as a whole, as well as attending to issues of professional competence (Lewis, 1987). Much also needs to be done to develop effective methods of supervising and supporting the practicum, particularly in the professional work setting, and to foster reflection, whether through tutorials, the practicum, profiles, learning contracts or professional diaries/journals (see Murphy and Reading, and Gillies, below).

It is also important to recognize that such teaching and learning methods may be particularly demanding in terms of staff time and teaching and counselling skills. The increasing pressure on resources, as a consequence of the expansion of student numbers in higher education without significant extra funding, may thus have particular implications for professional courses. New approaches to learning resources will have to be initiated, such as learning packages to support independent study, a development which is also relevant to the growth of part-time, employment-based and distance learning modes discussed in Chapter 2. Nevertheless, as Hughes notes below in his discussion of customized distance learning for management education, the development of such resources can be both time-consuming and expensive, as well as requiring particular skills. Equally, information technology-based learning resources which both develop students' own competence in personal and professional IT needs and also utilize the independent study potential of IT, require considerable investment and staff training. The development of effective methods of teaching and learning, including their match to rapidly changing course models and modes, is thus now one of the most challenging aspects of professional education.

Assessment

Many similar points could be made about assessment. Issues include: the implications for assessment of the development of integrated, topic- or problem-based course elements; the new emphasis on professional competence, particularly within the practicum; and the growth of different modes of learning. Experience suggests that these developments are having a considerable impact on the content, modes and timing of assessment within professional courses. There seems to be a trend towards individual or group practical projects as a major way of assessing course elements which are based within the higher education institution, while the assessment of competence in the professional work setting is primarily based on specific competences or criteria, which may or may not be progressively staged. Such trends also include the development of student profiles which, in identifying and supporting student achievement and progress across a wide range of competences and course elements, have the added value of integrating each component of the course. In common with some of the newer approaches to teaching and learning however, these techniques are demanding of both expertise and time. It is, for example, important to specify detailed criteria for the assessment of projects and the assessment of each individual's contribution can be particularly problematic. The involvement of students in the assessment process, whether individually or in groups, through self and peer assessment, and profiling, is also a time-consuming process, the more so when participants may also include employers and other members of the professional community, for example in assessment of competences during a workplace practicum, or indeed in project or other course work.

The assessment of competence in the practicum is the prime focus of current debate, encompassing not only the problems of defining competences discussed in Chapter 2, but also questions of methods and grading. Issues common to all assessment, such as validity and reliability, are particularly acute for the assessment of professional competence through the practicum, due to the focus on action (including the implicit agenda of satisfactory professional socialization) and the changing nature of the professional practice environment. Subjectivity, for example, can be a major problem, which cannot be entirely overcome by external moderation of assessment since the 'evidence', unlike written work, is not 'permanent' and cannot be exactly replicated for the moderating visit as the activities and contexts of any instance of practice are unique and forever changing. Although systematic triangulation can be helpful, for example, between student, institutional and practice tutors or mentors, or tutors and moderator/examiner, this again is time-consuming. As Murphy and Reading discuss below, such issues also have implications for the grading of practice. Although it may be relatively easy to assess the overall difference between 'pass' and 'fail', it is equally important to attend to a complex range of developing competences, and to the consequences of student failure, irrespective of whether fine grading is used or not. Nevertheless, the use of a range of evidence and participants, together with recognition of the inevitable role of informed judgement, can do much to ensure a system which is as rigorous and fair as possible.

Learning environments and partnerships

Professional education also requires particular attention to be paid to the learning environment, both physical and human. In addition to the need for appropriate environments for workplace practica, many professional courses require dedicated, specialized accommodation, which can be used to simulate the professional setting or otherwise provide a suitable context for professional learning, whether this is a studio for architects, a training restaurant for hotel and catering management or a model classroom for teachers. The immense pressures on space in most higher education institutions, due to expansion of the student population amongst other factors, make it extremely difficult to continue to justify, or at least have exclusive possession of, such dedicated accommodation. In addition, mature and CPD students in particular, together with employers paying for courses, may have certain expectations about the general quality of rooms and services, which, as noted in Chapter 4, now include higher and higher 'gold standards', particularly in the conference market. The pressures on students to develop the professional role in a demanding and complex practicum, or the different, but no less acute pressures on the part-time student who still has the responsibilities of a full-time job, also require a particular form of human environment, including both peer and staff support (Youll, 1985).

It is therefore important to ensure that student/staff partnerships are developed within which students can increasingly negotiate and take responsibility for their professional development. Nevertheless, such partnerships will inevitably be subject to strain from time to time, partly because of the demands of courses or the processes of assessment and also because of different student, staff and sponsor expectations. These, in turn, may vary considerably both across professions and from pre-service to CPD courses. As noted in Chapter 1, and by Gaunt in her case study in Chapter 4, there may be a number of tensions, as well as opportunities, in the triangular relationship between students (clients), sponsors (employers and other bodies) and providers (institutions), within which educational aims and practices, professional requirements and personal aspirations, have to be negotiated. Moreover, the increasing focus on monitoring and evaluation, in the interests of quality assurance and economic efficiency, raises all of these issues in special ways. Apart from the importance of evaluating courses within the higher education institution, to improve the quality of the student learning experience, in ways which allow students to express their needs and views and which give appropriate feedback on teaching (e.g. Gibbs *et al.*, 1984), the monitoring of employment-based and distance learning raises a number of new issues (see Hughes, below). Nevertheless, appropriate course design, allied to creative and effective methods of teaching, learning, assessment and evaluation, have considerable potential to overcome some of these problems, and indeed will have to be developed if quality is to be maintained in a situation of increasing demands on limited resources.

Conclusion

However, although many aspects of course delivery and assessment do need further consideration, it ought to be recognized that much professional education is at the 'cutting edge' of important new trends in higher education as a whole, including the development and assessment of competence, the growing interest in PBL and the increase in open and employment-based learning. It is thus very important that the HE institution fosters such initiatives, through programmes of staff development which can both bring together the theory and practice of adult learning/higher education and professional education and also facilitate the sharing of innovative and effective approaches to teaching, learning and assessment. Attention also needs to be given to the provision of appropriate learning environments and to providing investment for new resources, for both institution-based and other forms of learning. These issues will be considered further in Chapter 4.

The case studies below also illustrate many of the themes which have been discussed. John Astley gives more detailed consideration to the teaching of academic disciplines, arguing in particular the ways in which sociology can illuminate professional practice itself. Richard Hayward discusses the role of the architectural design studio, which crystallizes some of the issues involved in developing institution-based practica, including the need for dedicated space. Steve Hughes outlines some of the advantages and problems involved in developing distance learning for employment settings. Some of the methods and questions surrounding the assessment of competence are considered by Kathy Murphy and Paul Reading, who compare and contrast the approaches of two particular professional courses. Finally, Clare Gillies reports on some of the discussion, and practice, which has taken place in Oxford Polytechnic concerning the use of professional diaries in assessment.

Notes

1. I would like to thank David Jaques, Head of the Educational Methods Unit at Oxford Polytechnic, for his advice in preparing this chapter and for his comments on earlier drafts.
2. It remains debatable whether PBL can, or indeed should, be used as the primary/exclusive means of learning, and how student-centred it should be in terms of choice of problems, given the current emphasis on developing particular competences, limited staffing and other resources and the continued value of other methods to teach particular knowledge and skills. Nevertheless, the framing of learning in terms of practical problems which are or will be encountered by students does support much of the rationale of the post-technocratic model of professional education.

References

Akinsanya, J.A. (1987) 'The life sciences in nurse education'. In Davis, B. (ed.) *Nursing Education: Research and Developments.* London: Croom Helm.

Boud, D. (ed.) (1985) *Problem-Based Learning in Education for the Professions.* University of New South Wales, Higher Education Research and Development Society of Australasia.

Boud, D. (1988) *Developing Student Autonomy in Learning.* London: Kogan Page.

Brown, G. and Atkins, M. (1988) *Effective Teaching in Higher Education.* London: Methuen.

Cawley, P. (1989) 'The introduction of a problem-based option into a conventional engineering degree course'. *Studies in Higher Education,* **14**(1), 83–95.

Gibbs, G. (1987) *Learning by Doing.* London: Further Education Unit/Longman.

Gibbs, G., Habeshaw, S. and Habeshaw, T. (1984) *53 Interesting Ways to Appraise Your Teaching.* Oxford: Technical and Educational Services Limited.

Glover, I.A. and Kelly, M.P. (1987) *Engineers in Britain: A Sociological Study of the Engineering Dimension.* London: Allen & Unwin.

Goodlad, S. (1984) *Education for the Professions.* Guildford: SRHE/NFER-Nelson.

Jaques, D. (1984) *Learning in Groups.* London: Croom Helm.

Jarvis, P. (1983) *Professional Education.* London: Croom Helm.

Knowles, M. (1978) *The Adult Learner: A Neglected Species,* 2nd edn. Houston, Texas: Gulf Publishing Company.

Kolb, D. (1984) *Experiential Learning: Experience as the Source of Learning and Development.* Englewood Cliffs, New Jersey: Prentice-Hall.

Lewis, I. (1987) 'Teachers' school-focused action research'. In Todd, F. (ed.) *Planning Continuing Professional Development.* London: Croom Helm.

Neufeld, V. and Chong, J.P. (1984) Problem-based professional education in medicine'. In Goodlad, S. (ed.) *Education for the Professions.* Guildford: SRHE/NFER-Nelson.

Rogers, A. (1986) *Teaching Adults.* Milton Keynes: Open University Press.

Rowntree, D. (1981) *Developing Courses for Students.* London: McGraw-Hill.

Schön, D.A. (1987) *Educating the Reflective Practitioner.* London: Jossey-Bass.

Wattley, L.A. and Muller, D.J. (1987) 'Teaching psychology to nurses'. In Davis, B. (ed.) *Nursing Education: Research and Developments.* London: Croom Helm.

Youll, P. (1985) 'The learning community'. In Harris, R.J. (ed.) *Educating Social Workers.* Leicester: Association of Teachers in Social Work Education.

CASE STUDIES

Knowledge and Practice

John Astley

As identified earlier in this book, the conventional models of professional education in higher education are the technocratic and post-technocratic models. This in turn is part of increasingly practice-focused developments in professional education in many, if not most, professions at the moment, a factor which has much to do with the relative status given to 'academic' knowledge compared with 'practice knowledge'. The debates around the relative value of these knowledges is in turn the site of ideological struggles: which should be the more important in shaping the education of the practitioner? This case study will first discuss some general issues of knowledge and practice which have been the subject of debate at Oxford Polytechnic, and will then illustrate such issues with particular reference to the teaching of sociology on social work and health care courses.

One of the most significant aspects of such debates is the replacement of any one orthodoxy or conventional wisdom with another equally dominant one. There are also dangers in orienting education programmes to professional practice if the nature of the practice *itself* is not seen as problematic. Even where professions, or at least those associated with preparation for professions, are actively questioning the nature of knowledge, values and practice realities, they tend to overlook the problems of received ideas and conventional wisdoms. The professions which have developed even a broad range of motivations for practice, and where there are a variety of practice styles, still encourage the individual members of the profession to practise within an accepted and acceptable range. This has much to do with the current vogue for competence-related curriculum design.

One of our main aims in developing the concept of 'reflective practice' in education for professional practice is to challenge and question the nature of orthodoxies acting as social control. For example, one tendency in profession practice education has been for practitioners to consider their own and the profession's agenda before that of the client's, actual or potential. One of the paradoxes of professional education is that practitioners

are encouraged to develop a critical awareness of the context of their practice, and the problems of their clients, while at the same time the notion
is perpetuated that the professional practitioner is an autonomous, free-
thinking agent.

Another dimension of professional education that has to be considered
is exactly how do practitioners learn their practitioner role? If certain interventions are to be made into their conceptualizations of practice, we need
to know how people do understand their role and see the conditions of
their practice. (A similar point can be made about courses with less explicit
vocational outcomes in that academics working on undergraduate courses
intend to 'produce' able and insightful practitioners of that discipline or
vocation. For example, biology staff aim to have able, competent biologists
at the point of graduation and historians are similarly 'produced'.) So
whether we explicitly put the question of 'practice' at the centre of the
curriculum or not, that is where it is in reality in ensuing debates and
arguments. A profession, or indeed, a discipline, not only has a practice; it
also has a theory of action in which that practice can become reproducible,
valid technique. This means that professional educators not only deal with
questions of teaching technique to their students but also in teaching the
methods through which behavioural worlds can be created in which techniques can work. Our students thus need to know how to create the best
environments for their practice (Astley and Woolley, 1990).

However, how much of what we do as teachers is genuinely reflective in
this sense? We are all theorists and our conceptual worlds contain theories-
in-use, ideas about effective work practices which address questions like
'which approaches work well in particular contexts?' This involves us in
seeking explanations about why they work well and leads us to a readiness
to alter ways of working as dictated by recognizable changes in circumstances.
Developing our theories-in-use acknowledges that contextual complexity of
work settings and problem solving. These processes of critically reflecting
on our actions also go beyond the cognitive into realms of artistry (Schön,
1983). They are intuitive, improvisational and creative. Indeed much of
what we produce is symbolic creativity in a very everyday way.

However, our own theories may well be somewhat different from, and
perhaps come into conflict with, the espoused theories of our particular
profession or educational hierarchy. Thus it is often the case that practitioners will claim to embrace the 'public' espoused theories of their cultural
grouping while actually continuing to practise according to their own criteria. Such espoused theories also often remain the unquestioned and
unchallenged conventional wisdoms that practitioners may associate
themselves within a very tortuous way. Conflicts such as these therefore
need exposure and discussion, with the aims of reflection upon and improvements in our practice, and thereby our service to society. Considerations
of these value orientations often focus on practical questions of who should
teach what and where should this learning/teaching take place? One of the
characteristics of a large number of professional education courses is that

they borrow very heavily from other professions' bodies of specialist knowledge, such as the social or natural sciences. Indeed the regulatory bodies for most professional education insist upon courses including such interventions into the curriculum. Part of the contradiction for these occupational groups is therefore that they argue for the need to include such knowledge in a professional course, a clear expression of the overlap of the technocratic and post-technocratic models of professional education, which may also represent a pragmatic response to changing knowledge status hierarchies.

The gradual upgrading of professional education, from certificate to diploma to degree for example, is seen as a positive step towards achieving full professional status. However, this raises unresolved questions about the relative status of knowledge bases that make up the curriculum, as well as the relative status of theory and practice. How can professions achieve their educational aims? Should they keep the specialist academic bodies of knowledge in their courses, separately marked out in the curriculum, but taught by the host practitioners themselves, i.e. nurses, midwives or social workers teach psychology or biology? This is certainly relevant when an increasing number of professional practitioners acquire degrees in 'academic' disciplines. Or should they get psychologists or biologists to teach (have real control over) these specialist bodies of knowledge? Even when such problems are resolved, how are these bodies of specialist knowledge to be taught? What needs to be learned and how? What decisions will be taken over appropriate learning environments and who will have the final say over assessment? This involves questions about similarities and differences between courses and whether they are epistemological, functional to the particular course or social, in terms of the organization of the knowledge/discipline group. It also raises questions about the relationships between research and practice, the relative status of 'academic' and 'professional' knowledge and the social relationships between the various staff involved (see also Chapter 5).

Issues of knowledge (and power) relationships between staff and students are also pertinent. In a formalized professional education context (as discussed by Bines, above) it is also essential for the educator to take into consideration the debate on learning and cognitive styles. The 'reflective practitioner' should give due consideration to the ways in which interaction between teachers and learners takes place. Such questions are relevant both to the role of the academic specialists, those who are not members of the profession in question, and that of the professional practitioners themselves. Whether the aim is to introduce students to new skills, tasks or ideas, or to advance or develop the skills of existing practitioners, we also need to consider in what ways such things become less part of the teacher and more part of the student. Lying behind such concerns is the possibility of the imposition of a body of cultural and professionally sanctified knowledge and practice, particularly in a predetermined curriculum delivered regardless of the existing status, knowledge and experience of students. Our orientation could be different if we started from the premise that people of varying status in these professional education situations already know and do a great deal. They may have quite well-developed ideas of their own or as a group about what they want to do and how they feel is the best way to do it. Drawing on Knowles (1973) and others, do we adequately recognize the active role of adult learners in the processes of 'their' education?

Knowledge and practice in professional courses at Oxford Polytechnic

As noted elsewhere in this book, lecturers who are primarily teachers of 'academic disciplines' make a number of contributions to professional courses. Life scientists, for example, teach on most of the health care courses while sociologists contribute to courses ranging from social work to management education (George, Chapter 5). In each of these courses, aims include the teaching of relevant aspects of the discipline to support students' developing professional knowledge and action.

Such inputs may be made in a variety of ways although they are increasingly being integrated into professional elements of courses. In the new Diploma in Social Work, for example, some formerly discrete elements of the social sciences, such as law, psychology, sociology and social policy, are largely integrated into modules which are based on the issues, principles and practices of social work. This could be seen to reflect a largely functional view of the role of social science in social work education, together with sociology's epistemological concerns with the nature of society and social institutions which are also a focus of social work practice. A similar approach is found in health care courses. In addition, other aspects of a discipline may have an impact on why and how it is taught. Sociology, as a critical and reflexive discipline, not only offers a particular approach to substantive topics, such as the family or health, but also has considerable potential in relation to the critical analysis of professional practice itself. It thus can play a special role in tackling some of the issues raised earlier, such as the relationship between knowledge and practice, the espoused theories of a particular profession and social relationships between professionals and clients.

The sociological debate around professionals' discretionary power is particularly interesting in this respect. In my experience, a good majority of social work students have very mixed feelings about 'having' and 'using' power. They would like to be optimistic about their use of power but they have doubts. A reflexive sociological approach to such issues can do much to elaborate such concerns and offer potential bases for both beliefs and practice.

Sociology can also be related to the developing professional role in the 'practicum'. In relation to critical examination of knowledge and practice, any teachers organizing and facilitating courses for professional practitioners are, or should be, engaged in creating 'models of practice'. This is done via theory and debates around bodies of knowledge appropriate to the practice in question, linked to some form of work or practice experience for the students to try out their skills, reflect on the theories espoused and be coached in the techniques and arts of practice. Teaching sociology on a social work course should reflect such principles. For example, it does not take long before students are asked 'what is the nature of the social on which you are working?' They may well respond in terms of the received ideas of their practice, in particular some form of pathological model of society or individualized human behaviour. However the aim is not to make the students feel foolish or inadequate but on the contrary to debate the conventions of their practice culture and suggest that a sociological perspective might seek to challenge assumptions, including of course the value of specialized knowledge included in the course! Certainly this is social control, but it has the positive dimension of the desire to create the necessary overall learning environment or 'practicum'. One key aspect of this is to recognize that debates about theories and received ideas taking place in the classroom or the laboratory are just as much part of this overall learning environment as anything else, and that part of the skill in designing and facilitating a course is to get the balance right. This may not be easy, especially if students are not convinced, via their own experience, of the relevance and interdependency of the different aspects, and often requires reflective and innovative approaches to teaching and learning.

As noted above, such relationships between knowledge and practice inevitably raise issues about the relationship between academic and professional knowledge, research and practice, and staff and students, including the role of the adult learner. Certainly my experience of 'mature' students on nursing and social work courses confirms the general pattern that such students may feel de-(life)skilled in general and experience bouts of doubt about the relevance of their past occupational practice. They can acquire the impression that by and large their previous experience is to be left at the classroom door and that this is an inevitable part of the teaching/learning contract. Thus any sociology (or other) curriculum needs to begin with an acknowledgement of students' existing knowledge, skills and experience. In the teaching of sociology, this will include acknowledgement of their existing skills and experience in managing the self and the social, and the set of theories which students may hold as a consequence of such processes. Learning strategies are designed to draw out such theories, while comparing and contrasting them to the range of sociological theories on offer. Students then not only have the opportunity to reflect on their own theories of action, seeing them for what they are, but can also make judgements about the relative values to be placed on other theories, without denying themselves as skilled social actors, or the possibilities for change.

Nevertheless, even with such an open and reflective approach to adult learners, and to the relationship between knowledge and practice, it can still be difficult to develop particular forms of learning, teaching and assessment. For example, in relation to the use of essays as part of assessed course work in social work and post-registration nursing courses, it is not easy to persuade students to reflect on, write about and reflect upon again, their practice experience. There appear to be two main explanations for this. Firstly students are concerned lest they should fail to comply with the 'academic' expectations of their course, since personal life, educational or work experience has taught them to devalue their own observations and assessment of the world. They also find it difficult to integrate a reflective evaluation of their own practice into the conventional essay mode of exposition. Course design must therefore focus on establishing a learning and teaching framework which facilitates a range of routes to knowledge and to data.

Relationships between knowledge, practice, students and staff are also reflected in debates about research. This can be illustrated by discussion on the development of the nursing and midwifery degrees, the Diploma in Nursing and the new Diploma in Social Work. There was resistance in all three cases to including a 'research module'. In two instances, it was the nurse practitioners who wanted to introduce the element of research early on in the courses, which was resisted as unnecessary by some life scientists who felt that the research element in their contributory disciplines was sufficient. In contrast, in the social work case, it was the social scientists who argued the need to establish some clear research guidelines for the course, giving rise to mixed reactions from the social work practitioners, some of whom felt this was not really a necessary set of issues or skills. The link in all three instances was the establishment of specialist professional knowledge together with the clear commitment of the protagonists for a curriculum ideology that 'came clean' with students about the nature of knowledge.

However, despite such tensions, discipline-based and profession-based staff can successfully collaborate on courses for the professions. Such collaboration however requires a particular view of the role of the academic specialist. They should be valuable not merely because of their specialist knowledge base but because of the relationship between that knowledge base and their practice *as a teacher*. An experienced teacher of a natural or social science, with a highly sensitized orientation and commitment to the practice and education of other professions, may justifiably be a member of a professional education team, particularly since this then avoids the segmented delivery of bodies of knowledge assumed to be relevant to professional practice in favour of a reflective practice which includes the content, teaching and learning of the course itself. The teaching of sociology in professional courses at Oxford Polytechnic does attempt to reflect both the broad and reflexive role of the discipline and such aspirations in relation to the role of the teacher. Although this may as yet be difficult to fully implement in practice across all disciplines and in all professional courses, debates on such issues are beginning to create the conditions for future realization.

Conclusion

A sociological perspective on all the above suggests that we are actually discussing the 'interaction order' of education for professional practice of whatever kind. Human beings, with all their public and private diversity and homogeneity, are being assessed as members of a professional/occupational culture. Issues of selfhood and social accountability are fairly clear. A consideration of the conditions of our practice is not an 'out there' abstract activity. As teachers and researchers engaged in the design, delivery, assessment and evaluation of courses for professional practitioners, we are also required to spend a significant amount of time and energy considering the *processes* of these educational programmes as well as the *product*.

References

Astley, J. and Woolley, T. (1990) 'Reflecting on the interface between learning and teaching'. *Teaching News*, 26, Autumn, Oxford Polytechnic.
Knowles, M. (1973) *The Adult Learner; A Forgotten Species.* London: Croom Helm.
Schön, D.A. (1983) *The Reflective Practitioner.* London: Temple Smith.

The Architectural Design Studio

Richard Hayward

This case study, based on experience in the largest School of Architecture and Centre for Urban Design in the country, argues for the studio as the essential learning scenario of architectural education. Easy reference to the benefits of the studio have in the past marginalized the other learning activities of students, to the detriment of education, architects and architecture. Yet at its best, the studio generates not simply a thirst for knowledge and understanding of the arts, science and technology, but also a truly reflective practicum.

The squeeze is certainly on architectural education. With unnerving logic government prompts revisionist thinking not by sponsoring research and debate, but simply by proposing funding cuts. And what a good target the subject is: forced recently from the cover of protectionist 'professional' practices and fee scales, neither art nor science, with no one clear discipline or body of knowledge, except perhaps the rather nebulous area of 'design'.

Yet the qualities that are architecture's potential undoing are also generally much vaunted educational strengths. For architectural studies have long been rooted in problem solving, project-based learning, multidisciplinary curriculum and developing reflective praxis, as well as demanding high levels of numeracy, literacy and integrative and synthetic skills.

The role of the studio

Before formal education became the norm in the profession, students studied by doing: office 'pupillage', supplemented by evening art and technology classes. In most cases, pupillage involved regular interrogations concerning the work of more senior assistants by a master. Some offices were managed like a classroom, and the nervous assistant brought his drawings to the principal's desk for comment and correction.

In England and Europe, architecture schools as the primary source of education became the norm for the professional classes in the inter-war period. At the centre of this education was the studio. Donald Schön characterized the current squeeze on architecture education and its detrimental effects on practice in 1987 (Schön, 1987, pp. 314–15):

> Superimposed on our basic picture of the institutionalized dilemma of rigor or relevance is a more recent complication: an uneven but nevertheless significant resurgence of technical rationality and an accelerating constriction of professional autonomy combine to squeeze out the very idea of education for professional wisdom or artistry. And this is happening just as some factions, in some schools, are becoming newly aware of the need for something like a reflective practicum . . . The more general form of the squeeze play is as follows: the growing power of technical rationality, where it is growing, reduces the professional school's disposition to educate students for artistry in practice and increases its disposition to train them as technicians. And the perceived constriction of professional autonomy makes practitioners feel less free to exercise their capacities for reflection-in-action.

Earlier, Michael Polanyi (1957, p. 206), from a background in chemistry, affirmed that 'all arts are learned by intelligently imitating the way they are practised by other persons in whom the learner places his confidence', and suggested the method of working in higher mathematics that parallels very closely a description of design which would gain substantial acceptance from academics and practitioners (Polanyi, 1957, p. 131):

> The manner in which the mathematician works his way towards discovery, by shifting his confidence from intuition to computation and back again from computation to intuition, while never releasing his hold on either of the two, represents in miniature the whole range of operations by which articulation disciplines and expands the reasoning powers of man.

In Polanyi's terms, much of the design activity is heuristic rather than systematic. 'Obsession' he says 'with one's problem is in fact the mainspring of all inventive power' (ibid., p. 127), and obsession is undoubtedly at the roots of design. Designers and students do take their problems to bed with them and face them throughout the day. What then, of the studio?

The teaching activities of the studio are varied. There is a tacit faith underlying the studio exemplified in the old adage: 'I learn and I forget; I see and I remember, I do and I understand.' Much of the studio dialogue is graphic: student and teacher compare diagrams. Underlying this dialogue is generally a broadly Socratic teaching method. The teacher seeks to cause the student to demonstrate and rationalize intentions, to demonstrate synthesis and even to legitimize proposals. At the same time she seeks to identify where teaching by demonstration and example is required – a quest for appropriate intervention. Personal styles vary. Students soon establish which studio teachers act primarily as 'enablers', helping them to achieve their own particular solutions and those who tend to guide students to a more limited range of designs that reflect the teacher's view of an appropriate solution.

Essential to this dialogue is an interplay of strictly functional concerns and the concerns of architectural artistry. The studio is for most participants the place for the only true design synthesis of architectural knowledge, skills, and artistry. The range of topics of discussion and utilization in any one studio lesson is very broad:

- What are the space requirements of the brief here?
- What are the activities to be accommodated, and what spatial configuration does that require?
- Do we need a particular orientation?
- What relationship does this space have to this other brief requirement?
- Is it close enough?
- Is there a sound insulation problem?
- How are you tackling it?
- What's over this space?
- Can you let columns occur in the space or will you have to deepen the structural beam?
- What do you want the room to feel like?
- How will you do that?
- Is it like the living room in Frank Lloyd Wright's Robie House?
- How does the building look from outside?
- How does it relate to the adjacent existing building?
- Where is the rubbish stored?

  And so on . . .

Bourdieu reminds us, in another context, that art 'always contains something ineffable', which in the case of architecture is always above and beyond the primarily rational programme: '. . . pure practice without theory', as Durkheim says (Bourdieu, 1977). In the studio, this often involves a mimetic response by the student, a communication between her and the teacher 'like the rite or the dance' (Bourdieu, ibid.). The danger is, of course, that this is not underpinned by knowledgeable articulacy, and both participants are seduced by the mysterious pleasure of the encounter. These situations may foster the tendency of architects and their work to being esoteric and self-referential.

Argyris and Beinart *et al.* (1981) characterize the range of relationships of tutor/student in three broad categories thus:

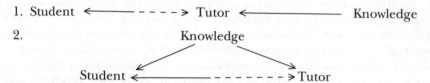

1. Student ←——— – – – –→ Tutor ←——————— Knowledge

2.   Knowledge

        Student ←——————— – – – – – – –→ Tutor

3. Knowledge

    Student ←——— – – – –→ Tutor

noting that the categories may be regarded as a progression from (1) the necessary early situation to (3) at the advanced level. Category (3) might be more fully expressed thus:

Knowledge

Student ←——————— – – – – –→ Tutor ←——————— Skill/artistry

although patently the student's skill/artistry development runs in parallel with the acquisition of knowledge, the practice of the former is the primary activity of the traditional studio class. The dotted reverse arrows indicate the learning potential for the tutor of every encounter, a point which my colleagues would not have me omit.

In all schools of architecture there is a considerable measure of peer group discussion about design. In some schools, studios are mixed in terms of experience and ability. This is sometimes arranged so that students are organized around particular design problems, or simply to work with a particular tutor or group of tutors. The educational arguments for or against this are little different to those for mixed age and ability group teaching elsewhere in the educational system. More exaggerated is the need for tutors to adjust to differing levels of technical and artistic experience in tutorial encounters. In teaching situations where general educational levels are roughly the same, there is perhaps more scope for group tutorials. In a studio arranged around thematically similar design projects, time can thus be saved, as in seminar discussions of written work. At Oxford Polytechnic, the undergraduate course is taught within year groups, whilst the two diploma years are taught as a single group. In both cases studios are generally theme based and group teaching is often used in addition to individual tutorials.

In the USA, tutorials are often called 'desk crits' whilst in the UK, the term 'crit', is usually reserved for what is sometimes called a 'jury session' in the USA. The latter is a more public event that takes place at the end of a design project and sometimes at a key interim stage. The crit is usually part of the assessment process and commonly involves teachers who have not been involved in the teaching process of the project – there is usually a more or less participating audience of peers and other students. However, the crit system generates considerable criticism from students. It is a confrontational situation. The 'rules' of the confrontation may often be unclear. Students frequently assert that they have been criticized and judged on areas of architecture that have not been a central concern in the design development. Like most schools, Oxford tries to avoid these tensions as much as possible; students are asked to write their own reflections on the conduct and content of the crit, for future reference by the student and staff. Most staff, whilst seldom wishing to be negative or discouraging, subscribe to Popper's dictum that whilst an organon of demonstration may be weak, an organon of criticism must be strong (Popper, 1972). Whereas the criticism of undergraduate students who produce architectural designs may be limited to areas of particular concern at a point in the learning process, graduate students may expect to be challenged to defend the totality of their architectural conceptions. At this level, the crit becomes, explicitly or implicitly, not only a vehicle for reflection on the achievements of the design process, but also a preparation for the design presentations which every architect in practice has to make to 'the team', the project leader, senior partners, 'the planners' or the patron/client. The primary criticism of final assessments by students is that much valid redirection takes place 'too late' for them to apply the lessons to their work. This is an affirmation of faith in the studio system and particularly in the value of wide debate of students' approach to design at a time when reflection and reaction may be used to reform the design proposals. A common criticism of architects and the architecture they produce is that their work is personalized and self-referential. Educational settings which face students only with introspective views of the subject are counterproductive for practice in a pluralistic world. Schools of architecture have to strive to represent a wide range of skills and views in the studio. The habits of reflective and responsive practice can only be fostered by confrontation and debate around the design acts of students.

Pressures on the studio

Some schools are on the point of dropping the 'one to one' tutorial in the early years of architectural education, because of worsening staff–student ratios. Others debate whether one or half an hour per week is feasible given staffing ratios and whether this is effective in architectural terms. Most graduate educational programmes work on a principal of 1:2 contact time to private study. In the sciences the balance is commonly more in favour of contact teaching time. Students in architecture generally spend about half their timetabled effort in the studio – say 18 hours or more during the timetabled working week. Inevitably given that the other 18 hours are of lectures and seminars, most of the studio time is without instruction. In reality, many, if not most, obsessive architectural problem solvers spend far more hours tussling with design. Of course much of this time is spent out of school, and many schools, Oxford included, struggle to provide good studio space and the 24-hour access to it, which many regard as ideal.

In the current debate centred on the scope and educational development of the architectural curriculum, outside observers express a difficulty with the apparent repetitive nature of the studio activity. In the past some schools have made great play with an increasing complexity over five years of architectural problems as a necessary part of progress through the course, say, from the house to the airport complex. More recently, this view has given way to a more balanced view that students may develop more performance skill with any but the simplest design problem. Zuk (1983) has drawn attention in this to the musical analogy. An essential part of music or surgery or architecture, is the development of analytical, synthetic, decision making and performance skills: practitioners need practice. Most professional practice situations are in fact effectively more complex than anything that can be simulated in the studio – and thus, most graduates who enter practice spend years under the supervision of consultants who have further developed beyond the master classes of the graduate studio to the level required by performance-based practice. School staff are properly under pressure to prepare students well for the reflection-in-action that the formative years in practice require – there is seldom time or opportunity to acquire these habits from practice unaided.

Saving the studio

It is debatable that pupillage was ever the ideal educational programme for architecture. In a profession that must serve a truly pluralistic and international clientele with technologies diversified quite as much as those employed in medicine, it is unthinkable that the design studio and the tutorial system should be abandoned without disastrous results. The quality of studio teaching could always be improved by an improvement in the quality of teachers, but as yet no plausible alternative has been offered to the regular brief encounter of every student with an accomplished studio master. The studio is a much maligned educational system that has offered much in its everyday working methods to current fashionable approaches to many less complex single disciplines.

In much of the rest of Europe and the USA, students are often permitted longer to complete their architectural studies. In the current education market, cheaper, shorter courses may well drive out the long, for all but the rich and privileged. However, paradoxically, at Oxford it is the specialist higher level programmes, beyond the basic diploma level, that are developing fastest, with very high proportions of overseas students. Let's hope that the 'squeeze' doesn't relegate the British architect to a technician role in an international market fuelled by British educated Masters students from elsewhere.

References

Argyris, C. and Beinart, J. (1981) *Architecture Education Study*. New York: Andrew Mellon Foundation,

Bourdieu, P. (1977) *An Outline of a Theory of Practice*. Cambridge: Cambridge University Press.

Polanyi, M. (1957) *Personal Knowledge*. Chicago: Chicago University Press.

Popper, K. (1972) *Objective Knowledge*. Oxford: Clarendon Press.

Schön, D. (1987) *Educating the Reflective Practitioner*. London: Jossey-Bass.

Zuk, R. (1983) 'A music lesson'. *Journal of Architectural Education*, Spring.

Customizing Distance Learning for Management Qualifications

Steve Hughes

The following presents the experiences of Oxford Polytechnic's School of Business in customizing the management qualifications of CMS (Certificate in Management Studies), DMS (Diploma in Management Studies) and MBA (Master in Business Administration) for large organizations. Specifically, the case addresses design and organization issues faced by the School in developing and delivering management qualifications by distance learning. Additionally it presents a 'model' designed for one major client, as a specific example of customization in action.

Introduction

The past decade has seen many organizations, in both the public and private sectors, being forced to take a close look at themselves, to re-examine the resources that make up the organizational 'being' and to check that these resources include the necessary tools and skills to take the company through the next decade. In an important sense, many of these companies are 're-discovering' themselves and in doing so seeking to provide their managers with nationally recognized management qualifications in an effort to improve performance, retain staff, and attract new staff in a diminishing recruitment market. Their approach has forced many educational institutions, particularly in the higher education sector, to re-examine how such qualifications are provided. The development and customization of distance learning programmes has been one result. The process is not without its problems but in our experience the ability of higher education institutions to respond flexibly and specifically to company requirements can be a fundamental factor in being selected as a providing partner. Companies are becoming more specific in their desire to meet the training and development needs of their managers and equally specific on the type of higher education institution they seek to build a partnership with. In doing so they are rejecting the 'life insurance' approach of those who present a portfolio of qualifications neatly packaged in designer brochures and offered as universal education panaceas that meet the needs of all interested companies. The resulting partnership can often require a heavy investment from both sides and demands careful planning, commitment, and clear understanding of each other's needs. Too often discussions are begun in earnest without taking stock of whether or not what is being discussed can actually be delivered in the time agreed and with the resources available. In cases such as these the result can be a hotch-potch programme meeting neither the needs of the sponsoring organization nor the manager it is designed to develop. The effect on the institution can include demoralized and demotivated staff, a reluctance to commit future resources to similar projects and an equal reluctance to develop organizationally in a rapidly expanding market.

Experience at Oxford Polytechnic

In 1987 Oxford Polytechnic, in cooperation with a large retail company, announced that a joint distance learning MBA would be developed which would be the first national management qualification at this level customized to meet the needs of a major company in the UK. The announcement stressed the partnership nature of the planning and design discussions between the two parties that would utilize relative strengths and experience. The primary motive had been a desire to design and deliver a high-quality, customized management qualification by distance learning which met the needs and requirements of both organizations and would provide the catalyst for similar cooperation in other related areas. The agreement would provide for the design and delivery of a certificate level qualification as a 'pilot' for the desired MBA.

Lessons from this innovative experience have been put into practice, by both sides, in the development of related and non-related programmes and projects. Oxford Polytechnic has now some of the most innovative distance learning programmes in the country and a School of Business recognized as a centre of excellence as a direct result. The company concerned now has a thriving in-house CMS programme and strong links with Oxford Polytechnic across the three levels of management qualifications. Some of these lessons and corresponding observations are presented here and serve merely to present the experiences of Oxford Polytechnic in this expanding field.

Distance learning: choosing a partner

In developing and customizing management qualifications using distance learning as the primary mode of delivery, the infrastructure of the deliverer becomes crucial. Rarely do educational institutions such as polytechnics and colleges have the necessary expertise and resources to develop distance learning materials from design to delivery, within a short timescale, and on a regular and flexible basis. The investment to develop such resources can be time-consuming and expensive both in the commitment of staff and capital outlay. Oxford tried it briefly and did not enjoy the experience. The alternative is to form a partnership with an organization that does have the necessary infrastructure and expertise. Many examples of such partnerships are now in existence, in Oxford's case with Wolsey Hall, Oxford for CMS and MBA levels, Kingston Polytechnic with Rapid Results and BPP at DMS and MBA levels respectively, Durham Business School with Rapid Results at MBA level. These are examples of relative needs and strengths being brought together to produce quality distance learning programmes flexible enough to meet the demands of particular company clients. Ultimately the academic quality of the materials and the programme lies with the educational institution, the production and design of materials with the distance learning organization. The development of this relationship, comprising a clear understanding of responsibilities and the recognition that regular communication minimizes potential areas of misunderstanding, remains crucial to the success of the enterprise. When the problem of infrastructure has been put to bed, the customization of a particular qualification can be addressed with more confidence; that is the confidence the institution has in its ability to meet the requirements of a particular company, and the corresponding confidence of the company that the institution can provide the necessary resources to meet its needs.

Customization

The process of designing the customization can be a very time-consuming and patience-sapping experience. Some companies approach institutions with little idea of what they are looking for. The resultant discussions can be very laborious and difficult as decisions are made, then unmade and goal posts constantly changed. Conversely, committing a considerable number of staff hours to a company training manager in designing a customized version of a much in demand management qualification and achieving complete agreement on the proposed model does not automatically mean the commitment of the organization. Having reached agreement with the provider, the training manager then has the task of convincing senior managers within the organization that the necessary budget and resources must be committed to the project. In short, convincing the training manager does not necessarily equate to convincing the organization. Recognizing this can minimize feelings of frustration as the time to contractual agreement lengthens. Many major companies are now beginning to appoint professional, innovative, training managers to examine and update their training and development provision. These managers have been given the task of examining their organizations' training needs, designing training programmes which meet these needs, and integrating them with nationally recognized management qualifications. At Oxford, working with such people has been a rewarding experience based upon professionalism, trust and a clear desire to design programmes which are best suited to meet their company requirements. Relationships such as these are a prerequisite to the successful customization of qualifications and are underpinned by a philosophy of partnership in the design and delivery of company specific programmes. Equally important has been the willingness to consider and take on board new innovations such as learning contracts, portfolio assessment, and the assessment of prior learning (APL), as well as distance learning and the traditional face-to-face sessions.

One example of this can be found in the design of a CMS level programme for a national building society (Figure 3.1) which takes account of different management profiles of those taking part in the programme. The distance

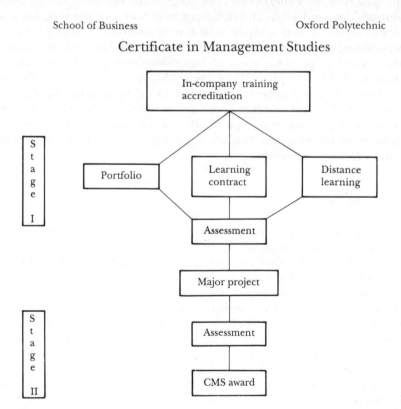

Figure 3.1 CMS level programme for a national building society

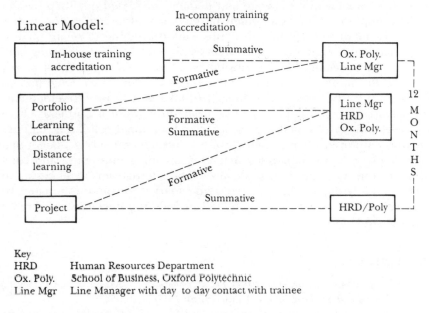

School of Business   Oxford Polytechnic

Figure 3.2 Assessment model for a large national company

learning route is the more structured and the more suitable for those with less managerial experience and responsibilities; the portfolio route for those with more experience in managing a variety of tasks and projects; and the learning contract route for those managers about to embark on a major work project for their company.

The area which perhaps best represents the philosophy of partnership is in the assessment process. Many companies pay only lip-service to the transfer of learning into the workplace. Little measurement takes place of what goes on after the two- or three-day course at the national training centre. Thus the cost effectiveness of the training in terms of improved performance, opportunities to practise newly acquired skills, or the dissemination of those skills to others is rarely monitored. Current programmes developed at Oxford seek to ensure that the transfer of learning is addressed and measured in both formative and summative assessment using line managers, training managers and Oxford staff. The process thus becomes a joint activity requiring commitment from both sides and not something externally monitored at predetermined times and places. To the manager on the programme the feeling of isolation sometimes experienced on programmes such as these is minimized as support is provided internal and external to the place of work. The assessment model developed for a large national company is an example of this (Figure 3.2).

Conclusion

As business organizations change and demand increased quality provision for their employees, correspondingly business schools are changing as they themselves adapt to meet new demands while struggling to retain quality. There is a danger that innovations such as distance learning, learning contracts and APL become the responsibility of a diminishing number of key staff with the motivation and commitment to develop such programmes. More staff must be actively encouraged to take part in new developments thus spreading a philosophy of innovation throughout a business school and developing it as a quality provider. The traditional belief that staff are only fully employed when presented with full teaching loads is a belief that has little place in a company-led market demanding innovation and commitment from staff and directorate alike. The alternative is to sit back and watch a rapidly expanding and rewarding market become dominated by those with the foresight to innovate and provide the necessary investment in labour and resources.

References

Bennett, Y. and McGoldrick, C. (1988) *Open Learning in Polytechnics and Colleges of Higher Education.* Huddersfield Polytechnic/MSC.
Mann, S., Binstead, D., Reynolds, M. and Sell, M. (1988) *The Effective Design and Delivery of Open and Distance Learning for Management Education.* Lancaster University/MSC.

Assessing Professional Competence

Kathy Murphy and Paul Reading

Grading practice: Nursing and midwifery

The Nursing and Midwifery course at Oxford Polytechnic commenced in 1989. If taken full-time, it is a four-year course, leading to an Honours degree in Nursing or Midwifery. There is a commitment to grading practice and a scheme for doing so has been developed. All practice modules from year 2 are graded.

Why the decision to grade practice was made

One of the tenets of the degree in Nursing and Midwifery at Oxford is that practice is central to the course. Practice modules constitute 50 per cent of the course. The course planning team argued that practice modules should be graded so that the overall achievement of the student would be reflected in the class of degree achieved. It was felt that without the inclusion of practice modules in the degree class system, its importance might not be recognized by students who, if only graded for theoretical work, might neglect practice and concentrate their efforts on theoretical modules. The consequence of this was a decision to grade practice modules.

Why it was felt that grading practice could be achieved

The difficulties of grading practice have been recognized by many educationalists (Hayter, 1973; Wood, 1982; Ross, 1988). Issues of subjectivity (Wysocki, 1980), lack of reliability (Hayter, 1973), and the changing nature of the clinical environment (Wood, 1982) have hampered efforts to grade practice fairly. The decision to grade was therefore not taken lightly; however, it was felt that grading practice was possible because of the following reasons. First, lecturer practitioners, who normally are the module leaders for practice modules, are based within clinical units and are accountable for standards of nursing practice, the quality of the learning environment, facilitation of mentors, and the assessment of students within their clinical units. Second, students are supernumary and are directly supervised during practice by mentors and lecturer practitioners.

Grading: Developing the system

An assessment group was set up with representatives from all the nursing and midwifery fields. The task of this group was to develop an assessment scheme, the work being divided into three sub-tasks:

- to identify competencies that the student must achieve
- to develop an appropriate assessment form
- to develop a grading scheme.

The competences were identified using Donabedian (1969) and Carper (1978) as a framework. They were divided into four levels which roughly equate with the four years of the course for full-time students. When developing the grading scheme, certain factors were taken into account. Firstly, there was a need for written evidence to justify the grade awarded which could later be used at internal and external moderation. Secondly, it was felt that reflection on practice by students should be incorporated into the assessment process, as this was felt to be a key element of learning in the practice situation. Thirdly, the grading scheme should be student-centred.

Grading in practice: How it works

On commencing a practice module the student is asked to identify his/her strengths and weaknesses in relation to the module. He or she then negotiates a learning contract with a mentor and lecturer practitioner. The triangular relationship involving the student, the mentor and lecturer practitioner is important in the whole assessment and grading process. The learning contract is designed to build upon strengths and weaknesses and the student specifies objectives which reflect personal learning targets and competences to be achieved. Resources and strategies for achieving objectives are also identified. Students are required to provide evidence from practice situations of achievement, and should therefore keep a written record of their practice throughout the experience. When a student feels that an objective has been met he or she writes the evidence of achievement, and reflections, down on the learning contract. This evidence is drawn from practice situations and a student can choose to write about those which he or she feels best reflect personal achievements. This is then validated by the mentor or lecturer practitioner. At the end of each practice module, the student, the mentor and the lecturer practitioner will meet to discuss the final grade. To aid their decision a profile of what can be expected from a student at each grade has been developed. The profiles have been developed taking into account the competences that must be achieved and the quality of the student's reflection. At the end of a practice module, all lecturer practitioners involved meet to 'justify' the grades awarded and these will be moderated by this 'expert' group. The learning contracts are available for external examiners to view, and lecturer practitioners can be available to justify the grade awarded if necessary.

Evaluation of the grading process takes place at the end of each module and at the end of each academic year and it is anticipated that refinements will be made in the light of experience.

A non-graded system for assessing competence in social work practice

In contrast to the relatively new nursing and midwifery course, the social work course at Oxford Polytechnic is well established as a generic, non-graduate course catering for a wide range of mature students. Although designated non-graduate, graduates may apply and approximately 30 per cent of students have a first degree or previous professional qualification. Practice placements are for a minimum of 50 days and are located in a variety of social work and community work agencies. The main tool for assessing practice competence is called an 'assessment schedule' and it is the operation of this schedule which is the main focus of this section.

The assessment schedule was originally put together by a small group of lecturers, practice teachers and students. It was approved by both internal and external validating bodies (CCETSW, 1981) and has the capacity to be modified as circumstances change. The schedule is divided into several sections, preceded by an account of the student's work during the placement written by the student. Completing the main body of the schedule is the responsibility of the designated practice teacher, but this is done in conjunction with the student. The practice teacher is not required to make any formal grading, but makes a clear signed statement as to whether the student's work has been satisfactory.

As with the nursing degree a key element of the whole process of assessment is the triangular relationship involving the student, the agency-based practice teacher and the polytechnic-based tutor. The tutor arranges the placement and after an initial meeting at the agency involving the three parties, it is the tutor's responsibility to prepare a written working agreement or contract for the placement. This includes the provision that the assessment schedule will be used and the date when it should be completed. All parties have a blank schedule given to them at this point with encouragement that it should be used as the placement progresses, not just at the end when the due date has been reached.

The idea that the schedule should be used throughout the placement, not just at the end, is based on an important educational principle. The process of reflecting on your developing knowledge and skill as you are learning to work in a new field is as important as being able to judge the level of competence at any fixed point. The assessment schedule has the capacity to be used both as an aid to this process of reflective learning and as a tool for the final assessment event. One of the key roles of the tutor is to guide both student and practice teacher in how best to undertake these two tasks.

One feature of the assessment schedule which has evolved in recent years has been the encouragement to provide evidence for the points that are being made in it. It is now based on direct observation, on joint work, on use of video and audio tape, and on discussion with colleagues, as well as using the student's written records. The clear expectation to use direct evidence has helped the whole process become more open and less secretive.

Another significant development has been to complete the assessment schedule at the same time as the student completes the final piece of written work, a social work study. In this the student writes a description and critical evaluation of one piece of work undertaken in the placement. Not only are students provided with guidelines for this but they know in advance the criteria which will be used for marking and how many marks will be available for each section. It is interesting to note that this piece of work has gradually become subject to a more structured grading system while the assessment schedule has remained an upgraded method of evaluation. The most important point is that set alongside each other, these two approaches to examining a student's level of understanding and competence seem to work. The assessment schedule and social work study complement each other and provide evidence of competence that is acceptable to external examiners, to internal assessors, to practice teachers and to students themselves.

Conclusion

Three common issues to come out of examining two different assessment schemes are:

1. The quality of the assessor is as important as the effectiveness of the assessment tool. Both courses are concentrating on this in their current developments and find it essential to put time and energy into both training and support for mentors and practice teachers, who need to be both committed and well prepared.
2. The complex nature of any assessment scheme whether graded or not. Nursing and social work are multidimensional professional activities which take place in a wide variety of settings. The assessment process has to do justice to this complexity and variety yet provide a scheme that is understandable, manageable and fair.
3. The process of assessment is an important component to building the competences required. Both courses value the concept of the reflective practitioner and see the assessment process as one way of helping this quality to develop.

Some specific concerns that relate to both courses are:

1. *Validity and reliability.* In making professional assessments, personal beliefs and biases are bound to influence judgements of competence. This raises questions about the validity of a particular assessment but it also acknowledges that professional practice in nursing and social work is not just about outcomes. It includes personal judgements about skills in human relations which are bound to have a subjective element.

   Both courses acknowledge this dilemma and see the development of clearer competences and assessment criteria as important ways of lessening personal bias. As practitioners become more experienced at assessing competence in students, and a dialogue develops between different disciplines in the caring professions, so reliability should improve. It is also helpful that during any student's time on the course, assessments will be made by different people in different contexts.
2. *Coping with failure.* This is a particular concern on courses such as nursing and social work where students feel themselves to be judged as a person as well as a professional. Both courses consider it important to allow students extra time to demonstrate their competence, but this extra time must be within clear time boundaries. Clearly a profession and its patients or clients must be protected from incompetent practitioners and there have been criticisms in the past when this has been in doubt (Brandon and Davies, 1979). On the other hand, the judgement that you are not good enough to be a nurse or social worker can leave an individual exposed and vulnerable. Helping someone adjust to failure is an important responsibility of the course and the personal tutor.
3. *Allowing for informal assessment.* A final concern is that some space is allowed for feedback that is not automatically included in the formal

assessment process. Working as part of a team is a useful way of enabling this, as students can obtain observations about their work from a range of people which can add to the reflective process of self-evaluation. Such informal interactions are an important part of the process which helps students to qualify with those two linked attributes – personal confidence and professional competence.

References

Brandon, J. and Davies, M. (1979) 'The limits of competence in social work'. *The British Journal of Social Work*, **9**, 3.

Carper, B. (1978) 'Fundamental patterns of knowing in nursing'. *Advances in Nursing Science*, **1**, 13–23.

CCETSW (1981) *Guidelines for Courses Leading to the CQSW*. London: CCETSW.

Donabedian, A. (1969) 'Some issues in evaluating the quality of nursing care'. *American Journal of Public Health*, **59**(10), 1833–6.

Hayter, J. (1973) 'An approach to laboratory evaluation'. *Journal of Nursing Education*, **12**(4), 17–22.

Ross, R. *et al.* (1988) 'Using the OSCE to measure clinical skills performance in nursing'. *Journal of Advanced Nursing*, **13**, 45–56.

Wood, V. (1982) 'Evaluation of student nurse clinical performance – a continuing problem'. *International Nursing Review*, **29**, 11–18.

Wysocki, R. (1980) 'Evaluation of student nurse clinical performance'. *Australian Nurse Clinical Journal*, **10**, 5.

Professional Diaries and Assessment

Clare Gillies

The professional diary is a tool designed by staff teaching education, nursing and social work in Oxford Polytechnic to help to develop both the habit and ability in student practitioners to reflect upon and evaluate their own work. This case study describes the debate that engaged the three professional groups involved.

Although all three professions have structured hierarchies and lines of accountability, some of the most difficult tasks that the new practitioner will meet have to be undertaken without a senior practitioner being present, for example, a nurse encountering bereaved parents, a teacher with a disruptive pupil or a social worker with an abused child. The educational process must therefore address not only issues of rigour in the assessment of competence but also promote personal and professional responsibility. Conventional approaches to education and assessment involve college lecturers in setting standards and devising rules and methods by which standards are measured. They are essentially limited in scope and make assumptions about group learning that may fail to encompass students' evaluation of their personal achievements. Further, such a process, which gives to the lecturer alone the power to make judgements about standards, runs the risk of infantilizing the students and is unlikely to increase student confidence or the ability to act autonomously. The professional diary is a means of helping students to take responsibility for their own developing competence (Holly, 1984).

The diary is not intended to be a detailed account of the student's activities while on practice placements, although it may be no more than this before a student learns to use it effectively. The student is required to: record the task; clarify the objectives; discuss how he or she prepared to undertake the work; if the objectives were modified and why this was done and how. Further, students must record how nearly the objectives were reached, what they learned from the piece of work and what theories, ideas from literature and empirical evidence were useful. The student is also encouraged to identify feelings and emotions, and the reasons for these when taking on the task; to note, for example, any fears or reluctance and, once again, to try to pinpoint the source of this concern. They are also required to ascertain what more they needed to know to have been more competent, what skills were lacking, as well as areas of personal growth, and then to chronicle what they intend to do about the shortfall. It is not impossible that, by the time a student is able to use the diary in this way, then he or she is ready to qualify. However, the struggle to engage in this complex task, to identify skills and knowledge required and to critically evaluate personal performance, is a rich source of learning and helps the student to achieve a gamut of skills necessary for a reflective practitioner.

Professional diaries may become personal and reveal a great deal about the diarist. A student social worker befriending a child abused by its parents will, almost certainly, reflect upon his or her own experiences as a child and, possibly, as a parent. It may be that attitudes to tasks such as parenting will always be confused by values or experiences but students must learn to understand the effect of these on their performance and professional judgement.

The importance of a reflective and personal discussion of their own competence to students' development is not difficult to see. The nature of the documented discussion does, however, raise questions about the ownership of the diaries and about who has the right to read them. Does a college lecturer need, or have the right, to know about the sometimes personal struggle that a student may have undergone before assessing a child at risk, even if the struggle was essential to the quality of the judgement? If this dilemma suggests that the diary should only be a learning tool and not a tool of assessment, then how can lecturers ensure that they are used? It is hoped that students will reach a point when they accept responsibility for their own professional standards and the significance of the diary in these, but they may need encouragement, pressure even, to reach it.

Ways have been devised in the Polytechnic to develop the use of diaries and to help students to learn to use them skilfully. It is considered essential that clear guidelines and headings, with examples, are given in the first place. In seminars or group tutorials, students are expected to read aloud from the diary, touching upon but leaving out personal issues. They may report, for example, faced with a demanding, attention-seeking child in a class, that they felt over-punitive but report only that they followed in the diary an exploration of personal attitudes and experiences that led back to their early family life. It is expected, however, that students would expose themselves to a discussion about the steps taken to maintain classroom discipline and the attention of the other children while coping with the disruptive youngster. They would need to defend their stance, if necessary, with theoretical ideas and research findings. Debate continues at the Polytechnic about whether such seminars ought to be part of the assessment process. Peer group assessment, formal and informal, will be significant to this process. It is agreed, however, that the seminar leader requires sensitivity as well as professional knowledge to make this a helpful experience for all students.

Where the diaries form part of the formal assessment, as they do in the Post-graduate Certificate in Education, students are required to quote from them and use the information recorded to reflect upon the information and management of the learning experience in the classroom, but not to submit the document itself. Guidelines for use of the diary emphasize 'thoughts and experiences' and concentrate on the 'here and now' learning activity, to encourage reflection but not too much introspection. In all the disciplines, however, the supervisor or mentor of the student in practice is alert to the impact on the student of the practice components of the course and they may, but not routinely, encourage the student to seek for the source of any discomfort in him/herself.

The diary is a particularly valuable tool in practice-based teaching sessions. If students are routinely asked to record how they prepared themselves to undertake a task, how well they carried it out, what they did well, what could have been done better, and how they set out improving their skills, they will start to feel responsible for their own learning. The value of these issues being addressed in a diary is, of course, that students can see how far they have progressed and how earlier uncertainties have disappeared or better preparation for work promoted overall growth.

Professional diaries are valuable if they are part of a learning environment where, as far as possible, there are no hidden agenda and from the beginning there is a clear statement about the professional standards that are expected at every stage (Curnock, 1985). Assessment methods must be clear and certain. A practice curriculum has been developed by the lecturers for each of the professional courses which not only attempts to set out expected standards but also makes clear what the student is expected to be able to do at any given time. For example, at the end of the early part of the course, a social work student must be able to communicate well enough with anyone, regardless of their race, class, gender, to ensure that their request for social work help is met, but by the end of the course the student must demonstrate an ability both to mediate between people in conflict and to challenge discriminatory attitudes. Clear statements about expectations and competence safeguard the profession and also provide a measuring rod without which the diary would lack focus.

References

Curnock, K. (1985) 'Educational principles in educating social workers'. In Harris, R.J. *et al.* (eds) *Educating Social Workers*. Leicester: Association of Teachers in Social Work Education.

Holly, M.L. (1984) *Keeping a Personal and Professional Journal*. Gelong, Victoria, Australia: Deakin University Press.

4

Management Issues

David Watson

The clearest challenge to institutions developing professional courses lies in the area of *marketing*, for it is here that most traditional practice has to be adjusted and new methods adapted. However, an effective marketing strategy will soon founder if the *quality* and appropriateness of the product is not maintained. In addition to assuring quality the effective institution needs a coherent strategy for *monitoring and development*.

In this chapter we attempt to unpack these issues before moving to the *administrative dimension*, especially the balance of responsibilities and initiatives between institutions centrally and their providing departments and units, as well as the need for robust *information systems*. The case studies at the end illustrate a range of relevant problems in systems, modes of study, financial arrangements, marketing, staff development and teaching roles.

Marketing

Polytechnics and most public sector colleges do not approach the question of recruiting to professional courses afresh. Most have a distinguished record of vocational education, including links with providers in further education, as well as experience of courses recognized by professional bodies. In some respects, however, these recruitment activities are as 'traditional' as the marketing of general higher education to normally-qualified students: part-timers come on day-release courses from employers (principally to take Higher National Certificates and Diplomas) or in response to local advertisement of evening continuing professional development (CPD) type courses, and full-time students can enter degrees 'advertised' through the clearing-houses in the normal way.

Expanding professional courses, just like the expansion of general higher education, depend critically on identifying and serving 'new' types of students: not just those who have missed out on education to the various 'entry-level' qualifications (such as BTEC courses and A levels) but also to those for whom a professional qualification would represent a change of career, and to those who need mid-career updating or units of CPD. It is thus partly about new types of students on old courses, but also about old types of students on new courses and new types on new courses. This complex market can be structured by raising a number of questions:

1. *Who are the students?* Fundamentally they will be of two types: initial trainees and inservice. However, these categories have come increasingly to overlap as the professions become more sensitive to their training and updating needs. Many current 'professionals' may require skills absent from their own preparation which now form a part of initial courses.
2. *Who pays?* In some important respects this question is in the political arena. As alluded to in Chapter 1, there is a permanent battle between employers and government about who should bear the costs of providing, and sponsoring students to take, courses leading to initial professional qualifications. In the inservice/CPD arena the situation should be clearer but is not. The prime interest again should be that of the employer (who in most instances arguably receives the greatest benefit), but many if not most professions place the onus for finding course fees and expenses on the students themselves. Instances of professions, like the Royal Institute of British Architects (RIBA) who support both providers and students are rare, but may provide important precedents as issues of reaccreditation and renewable licences enter our professional culture.
3. *Who 'validates'?* Issues of professional recognition affecting course design and assessment are dealt with elsewhere (in Chapters 2 and 3). In marketing terms this question chiefly affects the relationship *between* qualifications. Expressions of concerns about the 'portability' or 'transferability' of qualifications or parts of qualification from one level to another, from one profession to another, or indeed throughout a professional career, have only slowly evoked a system-wide response. The Credit Accumulation and Transfer Scheme (CATS) sponsored by CNAA has a major role to play here, and the CNAA and BTEC have finally begun to discuss the proper articulation between their qualifications. The Open University has for long been a willing, if slightly inflexible partner (because of the large size of their units) in schemes of mutual recognition. Perhaps the boldest such initiative is that of the National Council for Vocational Qualifications (NCVQ), the goal of which is to recognize levels of skill and competence in all potentially 'vocational' qualifications. The Council, moreover, represents a powerful ally in the fight for appropriate resources. Its new chairman Sir Bryan Nicholson (a past Chairman of the CNAA) has recently gone on record to urge the government to legislate to force employers to train 16–18-year-olds (see 'Legislation urged on skills training', *The Independent*, 22 December 1990). Now the Council has embarked on a consultation about the extension of its work above 'level IV' (roughly equivalent to further education's

higher point) on into diploma and degree-level work. Their working definition of skills at this new level V is as follows (NCVQ, 20 June 1990):

> Competence in the pursuit of a higher occupation or profession – as an employee or as a self-employed person – including the ability to apply a significant range of fundamental principles and techniques, which enable an individual to assume personal responsibility in design, analysis and diagnosis, planning and problem solving. Extensive knowledge and understanding will be required to under-pin competence at this level, together with capability in management and supervision in executive and some professional fields.

It remains to be seen how this attempt to capture or legislate the qualities of a 'reflective practitioner' will play with educational providers at the level of higher education. At the lower levels attempts at counting competence have met resistance from employers and educators alike (Welsh and Woodward, 1989, 3.4.2). As one survey concluded, 'so much effort from the Training Agency and NCVQ have gone into stressing the vocational dimension that less attention has been paid to the wider [educational] implications' (Haffenden and Brown, 1989, p. 24). Similarly the Unit for the Development of Adult Continuing Education has suggested (UDACE, 1990, p. 2):

> The NCVQ concept of 'occupational competence' is closely related to a specific job role and sits uneasily in a degree programme designed to develop broad intellectual, creative and analytical skills, which can be employed in a wide range of jobs.

Other misgivings about what have come to be summarized as NVQs are set out in Chapter 2.

4. *Who are the other actors?* or *What is the competition?* In addition to educational providers and the professional bodies themselves there is a variety of bodies active in the field which see their role as facilitative. Many of these are arms-length agencies of government such as the Professional, Industrial and Commercial Updating Programme (PICKUP) of the DES, or the Department of Employment's funnelling of training money initially through the Training Agency (TA, now transformed into TEED – The Training, Enterprise and Education Directorate). Most of this latter largesse is now in the hands of a series of regional agencies called TECs (Training and Enterprise Councils) constitutionally designed to separate the commissioners and funders of programmes from the 'educational lobby' of the providers themselves. Institutions have to build sensible and productive relationships with all of these intermediaries as well as with the larger companies and employers now seeking to systematize and accredit their in-company training schemes.

Quality

In such a competitive arena providers have to take especial care to ensure that their policies on both prices and quality are optimal. (One of the great ironies about current government stances on professional and vocational education is that the encouragement to education, generally, to collaborate with industry is matched with devices to ensure that providers *compete* to sell a product which they have, ideally, collaborated to design and develop; this is only one of a number of ways in which a crude market metaphor for the educational process is inadequate.) Price (principally fees) is dealt with below. From the point of view of quality there are several variables which apply with particular force to post-experience and professional courses and which require institutional sensitivity. In general they cohere around the notion of recognition and supply of the special needs of such students.

1. *Staff development.* One major effect is upon expectations of staff and the resulting requirement for their development. Servicing professional courses has implications from recruitment and retention through to the teacher's own training and professional practice. In several such areas (notably teacher education) it is now recognized that prior experience of professional practice, by itself, is not enough. Staff not only need updating and refreshment in terms of their knowledge of current professional practice, but also require targeted assistance in terms of its translation to the educational setting. The teaching methods associated with identification of professional competence, the supervision of the 'practicum' and the encouragement of appropriate 'reflection' are all highly specialized, and apart from the normal experience of discipline-based teachers in higher education. Then there is the question of adaption to the learning environment. CPD students, for example, may require a particular approach, while, to realize fully the opportunities provided by more flexible modes of delivery, the teacher of professional courses needs 'hands-on' experience of accrediting prior learning, negotiating credit transfer and the like. Managers in this complex area should be of no doubt that in achieving high quality, staff and their development are the key resource.

2. *The curriculum.* As discussed in Chapter 2, design of professional courses is best achieved collaboratively with the professional bodies and their representatives. A marketing implication is that courses are best presented so that they fit with the structure and career ladder established by the better organized professions. A good example is the statement of levels developed by the United Kingdom Central Council for Nursing, Midwifery and Health Visiting project on Post-Registration Education and Practice. The UKCC separates 'practice following initial registration', from both 'specialist practice' and 'advanced practice'. The latter is concerned with (UKCC, 1990, p. 7):

adjusting the boundaries for the development of future practice, the pioneering and development of new roles responsive to changing needs and, with advancing clinical practice, research and education to enrich professional practice as a whole.

A parallel example is the Engineering Council's codification of the 'recommended roles and responsibilities' for the different levels of membership; progressively Engineering Technician, Incorporated Engineer, and Chartered Engineer (Engineering Council, 1990).

3. *Modes of study*. For all students other than those on full-time initial courses the chief requirement of course provision is that it should be flexible. At one end of the scale this can simply relate to timetabling, with, for example, parents with family responsibilities seeking to compress the time of attendance between 9.30 a.m. and 3.00 p.m. At the other end, part-timers may only make a range of demands after 6 p.m., or during weekends and traditional vacation periods. Fuller recognition of the needs of post-experience and professional courses will lead to courses becoming agnostic as to mode (with easy facility to move between full-time, part-time and distance or open modes of study).

4. *The learning environment*. Flexibility of course provision means, in turn, flexibility of support services. Again there is a spectrum of possibilities. For students on-site in the evening and weekends, a reasonable level of communal and catering facilities is a minimum prerequisite, including basic reception and security services. To assist productive patterns of study reasonable access to library and computers should also be provided. At the other end of the spectrum an expanded portfolio of post-experience and CPD courses, including higher level qualifications, apparently (in market terms) requires enhanced residential and conference facilities including the 'gold standard' of the 1990s: *en suite* bathrooms. This is all before consideration of the various manifestations of the 'practicum' such as the studio or the model classroom on site; the back-up to a student and/or supervisor in the field.

Monitoring and evaluation

Further rethinking is necessary in the areas of monitoring and evaluation. A traditional array of performance indicators for courses – qualifications on entry, retention rates, results, employability – may produce very misleading results when applied particularly to post-experience courses. The potential fragmentation of these courses, and the students' (perhaps idiosyncratic) use of them, is a strength and not a weakness. Even the concept of 'value-added' may require careful shading.

More robust measures will include the extent of collaboration with commercial, industrial and professional partners and the aggregation of the effects of increased qualifications and educational experience upon the career pathways and professional practice of individuals. A particular point of entry into the field of evaluation is via interprofessionalism, discussed in Chapter 5. Whereas much development of 'pure' or 'single' profession courses might be said to depend upon a creative tension between educationalist and the professions, in interprofessional areas it is frequently the 'academics' who hold the ring. In support, much of the research effort made by institutions in this area is appropriately in evaluating the effectiveness of both education and practice.

Administration

From a central perspective many of these issues reduce to patterns of management and administration which we have tried to explore in the case studies below. Again a series of questions exposes the dilemmas.

1. *Who is responsible for what?* Setting the right balance between institutional, departmental and course-based responsibilities for marketing and promotion in particular is a tricky task. The bottom line has to be the recognition that each level can add value to the others' efforts, and that if they contradict each other there will be disaster. Departmental actions are invariably set into an institutional statement of mission and strategic plan, but this will not by itself solve the key problem of how clients find their way smoothly and efficiently into the institution. The 'one-stop shop' is an attractive but difficult goal to achieve. Similarly, seizing new opportunities in a rapidly developing market (for example, in accrediting or customizing incompany schemes) requires quick and authoritative communication links between centre and course staff.

2. *Does it pay its way?* Setting fee levels is probably one of the most contentious issues in the internal dialogue about professional courses. Departmental or course-based sensitivity to the levels which the market will bear, often allied to a strong suspicion and resentment of the level and use made of central overheads, is often matched by a curious insensitivity to questions of viability (such as group size) and to the process of raising invoices and getting paid. In courses which attract a variety of clients with a range of abilities to pay, further noise can be injected into the system. In these circumstances some level of central discipline is vital. For example, on the question of fee levels it is far easier to assess costs, establish an appropriate fee and discount it for particular categories of customers (say, other public sector organizations) than to allow a proliferation of individual negotiations.

3. *Who keeps the books?* Historically a variety of course types has led in institutions to a variety of record-keeping systems, often inefficient and impenetrable to central audit. Setting up an institution-wide management information system for post-experience and professional courses buys a number of benefits, and not least some relief for the emerging class of tutor-administrators.

4. *Can we have it yesterday?* Planning and validation cycles in public sector institutions are rigorous, accountable, and established to march in step

with the slowest soldiers. They were characteristically fixed at a time when the institutions concentrated on full-time, linear courses, with a fairly uniform pattern of recruitment. Reacting creatively and effectively to the changing demand for professional courses requires new methods ('fast-track' approvals, delegated authority in contractual negotiations, and risk-taking) which are hard to reconcile with rigour and account-ability. Nonetheless, this circle must be (and in cases of best practice has been) squared if responsiveness and quality are to be simultaneously supplied.

Conclusions

These remarks have been written largely from a central perspective, as exemplified below in the case study by Stuart Brown on information systems. The other case studies show departments and courses interacting with each other and with the centre. Trevor Watkins considers the implications for departmental policy and management of responding to a rapidly evolving market for management education. John Glasson underlines the importance of financial know-how and responsibility, at central and devolved levels. Diane Gaunt elaborates the context within which the design, marketing and delivery of a portfolio of courses for practising teachers goes forward, emphasizing the management of change. The vital role of staff development in effecting change is then picked up by Ruth Champion, in her account of the emergence of the role of lecturer-practitioner in health care studies courses.

The desideratum from an institutional perspective is obviously a system with a high rate of synergy and a low level of noise. Keeping this goal at the forefront of the efforts of all of the participants is a difficult, but crucial, management task.

References

Engineering Council (1990) *Recommended Roles and Responsibilities: Chartered Engineer, Incorporated Engineers, Engineering Technicians.* London: Engineering Council.

Haffenden, I. and Brown, A. (1989) *Implications of Competence-Based Curricula.* London: Further Education Unit.

NCVQ (National Council for Vocational Qualifications) (1990) *Extension of the NVQ above Level IV.* London: NCVQ.

UDACE (Unit for the Development of Adult Continuing Education) (1990) *Learning Outcomes and Credits in Higher Education, Information Notes 1 & 2.* London: UDACE.

UKCC (United Kingdom Central Council of Nursing, Midwifery and Health Visit-ing) (1990) *Discussion Paper on Post-Registration Education in Practice.* London: UKCC.

Welsh, L. and Woodward, P. (1989) *Continuing Professional Development: Towards a National Strategy.* London: PICKUP/Further Education Unit.

CASE STUDIES

Marketing Management Education

Trevor Watkins

The spotlight of national attention has focused on management education in the recent past with the establishment of the Management Charter Initiative (MCI). Unfavourable reviews of management education in the UK were produced by Charles Handy (1987) which highlighted the international comparison with the UK's major competitors, showing a lack of MBA output and a surfeit of accountants in the UK. The Constable and McCormick Report (1987) criticized the 'ivory tower' elitism of much management education and suggested the need for more vocationally relevant courses.

Against this background the School of Business at Oxford Polytechnic devised a hierarchy of management course provision based on Certificate, Diploma and Masters levels. The principle behind the developments was that each course would aim to produce more effective managers, albeit at different levels in the organization. The Certificate would aim at newly appointed managers, the Diploma at managers with some management experience and the MBA at high fliers aiming for general management in senior management roles. A further principle in the development was to make the courses as accessible as possible, which led to a multi-mode approach made more flexible by using common content across modes. Thus, the School has management qualification courses available by attendance (full-time or part-time) and by distance learning at Certificate (BTEC CMS; CNAA CMS) Diploma (CNAA DMS) and Masters (CNAA MBA) levels, with content that matches each version.

Marketing these courses in an increasingly competitive environment is based on joint venture deals with Wolsey Hall, Oxford (CMS and MBA) and BPP Publishing plc (DMS) for the distance learning modes. There are essentially two markets: the individual market and the corporate market. Access to the individual market is increasingly expensive and commonly relies on mass media advertising, notably in the quality weekend national press. Such advertising is expensive and thus requires heavy investment in the process. Economics of scale (and scope) should apply and thus one expects the market to feature oligopolistic tendencies relying on non-price competition. A further issue with the individual market is the long decision lead time. In some cases the individual is funded by his/her employer and the process of gaining agreement takes time. Otherwise, the time and cost commitment by the individual is great, can affect family life and typically involves careful thought.

To offset the problems noted above, there is evidence of strong demand, particularly at the MBA level. The need to provide good quality case materials is a barrier which increases the cost of entry. However, a number of suppliers are present in the market which as yet shows no sign of abating. As already noted, one might expect to see an increasing concentration ratio. Thus, it is likely that the marketing costs of gaining extra students will rise, making this market segment less attractive and acting as a barrier to new competition.

Turning to the corporate market, there is more opportunity for market penetration, using the partnership route with large client companies. It is increasingly likely that this route will incorporate accredited, in-company training courses. Such an approach has the marketing advantage of tying the client company to one supplier.

There are a number of marketing problems involved in this process. Firstly, identifying client companies who might be interested is not an easy process. It is likely to be inefficient to use advertising and general mail shots are likely to have extremely low take-up rates. The most likely contact is based on personal contact which might be initiated by press reports of existing partnership links. This market is in an early stage of development and the returns from general attempts to contact potential clients are likely to be low.

A further problem is that typically a two-stage sale is involved. Initial contacts are with the personnel/management development function but the budget leads for the costs involved are likely to be controlled by the line managers of the specific participants. Thus setting up a deal with the personnel department is only the first stage in the proceedings. Frustratingly for the supplier, it is often the personnel department which has to sell the concept to the line managers. This process may well involve a board decision. Certainly it takes time and the lead time for such partnerships deals can extend to a matter of years.

If in-company training course accreditation is involved, the time factor is increased further. The process of accreditation is discussed elsewhere in this text but it is a process which is costly in time and money. One of the particular skills that polytechnics can offer is that of assessment. Typically, in our experience to date, companies are relatively poor in making formal assessments of students on in-company courses and there is often a need to bolster up this process where these courses become an integral part of the qualification programme.

There is also a wider issue. The MCI has focused attention on managerial competences and there is a need for forward looking management programmes to include more skill-based approaches which develop identified competences. The definition of relevant competences is more difficult, the less job related a course is. The assessment of competences remains a difficult area.

There are many marketing problems involved in management education. The market is increasingly competitive and sophisticated and typical signs of over-supply, such as niche marketing using product proliferation, are starting to appear. Only the early market entrants can hope to survive because of the economics of scale and scope factors noted earlier. Thus, management education is highly unlikely to provide the elusive pot of gold which many suppliers might suppose. Nevertheless, the potential benefits in terms of extending the catchment area, job enrichment for staff and closer links with industry, are distinct potential advantages.

The implications for business school managers of the increasing need to market management courses aggressively are legion. For instance, generating advertisement budgets on advance of income from courses is not a procedure which is used commonly in the finance processes in polytechnics. As SSRs have worsened, the time available for lecturing staff to spend on activities such as marketing to corporate clients and accrediting in-company programmes, becomes more difficult to find. Even a simple matter such as timetabling short courses for one or two days at a time is tricky when staff have regular timetabled commitments on qualification courses.

The benefits from establishing close working relationships with major employees can be great. The public relations benefits can initiate further enquiries from other employers. The staff development benefits from regular contact with organizations should not be underestimated.

The dilemma for the business school manager is similar to that for other commercial managers, namely how best to use limited resources to optimize sales. The need to build long-term relationships with organizations is a common business problem but one which until recently, educationalists, used to having a monopolistic buyer (central government), have not had to face.

References

Constable, J. and McCormick, R. (1987) *The Making of British Managers*. London: British Institute of Management/MSC/NEDO.
Handy, C. (1987) *The Making of Managers*. London: NEDO.

The Cheque is in the Post

John Glasson

Introduction/context

The School of Planning is deeply committed to post-graduate professional courses. Our post-graduate courses in planning, and in urban design, were originally introduced in the late 1960s and early 1970s. At that time the fledgling Polytechnic had about 2000 students and well over 200 staff. Today, in addition to the original courses which have been developed and diversified in many ways, the School has post-graduate courses in housing, historic conservation, environmental assessment and management – in a wide range of modes. We are still deeply committed to post-graduate courses – they account for 40 per cent of all student numbers – but the resources position has tightened greatly. The Polytechnic has 8000 students and well over 400 staff. The School of Planning is larger now than 20 years ago but the Student : Staff ratio (SSR) is much higher. So what are the management/administrative and resources issues involved?

Administrative and management issues

Crossing the administrative and management threshold

Oxford Polytechnic is well known for its undergraduate Modular Course. This now includes about two-thirds of all undergraduate students, taking either named Honours degrees, or Combined Honours programmes. The School of Planning tentatively dipped its toe in the modular pool via a share in the new single field in tourism introduced in 1987–88. The offering of our undergraduate planning programme soon followed and is now very successfully delivered in the modular format.

At the same time, a unit-credit approach was considered for our burgeoning array of post-graduate courses. This was partly as a move towards more resource efficiency, partly to improve student choice and partly to introduce more flexibility and ability to adapt quickly. Our post-graduate courses (see Figure 4.1) are all offered on a common unit-credit system, which is also compatible with the undergraduate scheme. There is sharing of certain units across courses, but, an important feature of all our programmes is the maintenance of a strong core to each course, reflecting its focus and giving a clear identity. Thus, the MSc in Planning Studies has core units in planning policy studies, research methods and dissertation; the Diploma in Planning has core units in planning law, management and finance, central issues in environmental planning and the implementation project. The core normally accounts for about half of the course; the sharing comes with a range of specialization routes across the programmes.

The common unit-credit approach has allowed us to move from a position where we had several free standing, but vulnerable, courses to one where we have an array of semi-independent, inter-linked courses. It can be seen as more complex, but it is certainly more robust – choices are real and courses run. We have crossed an organizational threshold: students are already reaping the benefits, and staff and the School as a whole should also gain. But what about the complexity of interlinking courses and introducing a wide range of choice?

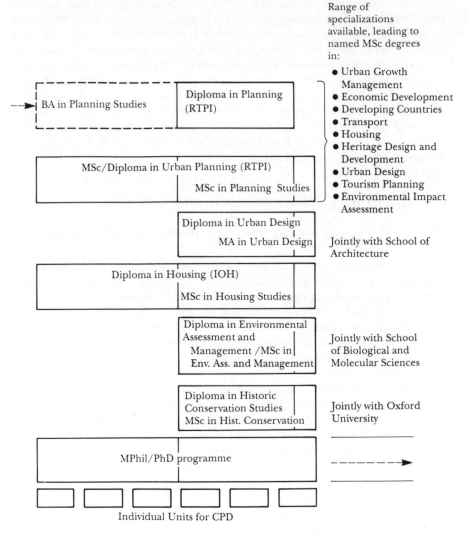

Figure 4.1 Oxford Polytechnic: School of Planning post-graduate programmes in unit-credit scheme

Local user-friendly systems

Our courses have a wide range of students – full-time, part-time, mixed-mode and CPD, from the UK, EC and from further afield. Each student must indicate his/her specialization choice and options for the chosen course well in advance. The core, as discussed, is predetermined. A standard application form, and some simple analysis, allows us to determine the size of the various unit-credit groups for the coming year. Students are informed of choices well in advance. Results are processed on a termly basis for our term-long units, and credits are accumulated in a logical programme of prerequisites. With over 300 post-graduate students on our courses we can operate with our own decentralized school system. Course tutors and a good secretarial team provide the user-friendly, flexible and, face-to-face approach which is important for such courses.

Which course am I on – is there an identity crisis?

The operation of our post-graduate courses benefits from varying degrees of commonality and sharing units, especially for specializations. The courses also benefit from a wide range of student sources. But a clear identity and ethos is maintained for each course, partly reflecting the requirements of professional syllabuses and partly the differing objectives of the various Masters and Diploma courses. As noted, each course has its own substantial core, and there are clear patterns of progression through a system of prerequisites in addition. Only limited access is given to advanced units in the compatible but undergraduate Modular Course in the Polytechnic.

The diverse range of students taking these courses can be one of the greatest strengths and attractions of such programmes, but the overall balance of the mix needs to be managed. Currently, one of the greatest dangers is of 'part-time swamping' of full-time students. Part-time students bring many attractive features to a post-graduate course – not least their day-to-day experience in relevant employment. But with the difficulties of funding of full-time students, there is a need to work hard to maintain the mix (this is discussed further, below).

Other management tools – the answer lies in the timetable

Too much choice and inter-linking can potentially be an administrative nightmare. Part-time student demands could sway courses in terms of what can fit on part-time days. Our response has been to operate some basic rules of thumb – applying minimum numbers thresholds to units and seeking to influence maximum numbers. The range of choice is also more tightly drawn for part-time students. There is also the judicious timing of units across the weekly timetable – as we all know, some times are more popular than others! This balancing of student choice and administrative reality leads neatly into a fuller discussion of resources issues. Do post-graduate courses pay?

Resources issues

The resource bill – getting into debt

In the built environment, the analogy of a construction project is apt. There are 'construction'/setting up costs and 'operation'/running costs – once the course is established.

Costing out a course review or new course design is an interesting exercise. In terms of staff time, it is easy to run up 'bills' of at least 500 to 1000 hours (£10 000 – £20 000 for a Masters programme); and then there is the opportunity-cost approach! From our experience over the last few years, with several major post-graduate development exercises, our unit-credit approach is producing more efficient course development. It provides a number of fixed points for any new course, a template, plus some existing units which can be utilized in new courses. Ironically, it has also revealed that designing new courses (including fundamental market research) is often more straightforward than modifying existing courses.

Our recent course developments (environment assessment and management; historic conservation) have involved inter-school (with Biological and Molecular Sciences) and inter-institution (with Oxford University) patterns of working. Much of the interest, opportunity and excitement of post-graduate course development is in exploring and developing the niche markets between the traditional areas. But such working can involve a coming together of widely different 'cultures' and approaches. Reconciling differences in a constructive way can take time, although from our experience, the unit-credit approach has been invaluable as a common language, and there has been a great deal of goodwill to work together.

The operational resourcing of a course is a key element in the design and validation process. Staffing costs are central and particularly with the lower SSRs we usually seek to build into post-graduate courses. Scale economies of shared units help; minima and maxima rules of thumb seek to avoid the excesses of choice. But of course, sharing and economies of scale can have logistical problems for size of rooms, seminar groups etc. – all of which need to be built into the costing. There is also marketing. Post-graduate courses invariably need a high profile; the 'semi-automatic' PCAS/LEA market of undergraduate courses is a different world. This marketing involves high costs (e.g. advertisements in the prestige national press and journals) and/or high effort in terms of targeting potential consumers. However, there are some 'free' outlets – new courses listings in some papers (e.g. *THES*) and in professional journals, and these are valuable.

Reaping the benefits

Why do we develop post-graduate courses? Are they good investments? You can look at the returns in several ways – some qualitative, some quantitative, although the distinction is not too clear at times.

Such courses can greatly enhance the internal and external reputation of a School. They often emerge out of staff research interests; they are often at the 'cutting edge' of the subject. They pioneer new frontiers and this can be invigorating and rewarding for all concerned. Post-graduate students bring an extra 'challenge' to staff; to get on courses they often need a 2.1 qualification at first degree level and they are usually highly motivated. New courses can achieve status in the various rankings (e.g. ESRC A Plus) and ideas can percolate through to other courses. Practice and research links may develop, especially in applied fields, bringing consultancy and research contracts to the schools concerned.

However, more mundanely, school and institutional survival depends on the full-time equivalent students (FTEs) counts and money. How well do such courses pay? They are often longer than undergraduate courses – up to 48 weeks in an MSc annual programme. Unfortunately, this may not be reflected in the FTE count, where the undergraduate mentality of 'all full-time students equal one' may still pervade. The FTE payback may be further eroded by a low part-time weighting of 0.4. We certainly need to relate full-time and part-time FTE allowances clearly together. Overall though, the FTE allowance, from my recent experience, bears little relationship to the work load involved.

The alternative is to take the money. Full cost courses will work in some markets, although with a bias towards the immediately relevant and applied professional courses. Full cost fees may provide a reasonable income for a course to run, assuming central overheads are not too draconian! There are also merits in a mixed economy; for example, trading off the inferior FTE allowance noted above, for a fee supplement. An enlightened approach by finance officers is needed, encouraging Schools to innovate. A traditional heavy hand can have a traumatic effect on innovation.

And then there is sponsorship. At the end of the day, a post-graduate course must generate students with funding for fees, and for the essentials of life. Research Council listing and funding can help, as can, for example, European Social Fund support, but the uncertainty attached to such sources is not a good foundation for course development. A market-related course may attract sponsorship from industry and the professions. For £6000–£7000 per year, a sponsor may achieve some free marketing, some in-course research, and a guaranteed employee. But obtaining such sponsorships takes time and effort, and often at Head of Department level. The ultimate form of sponsorship is 'self-sponsorship' by private funding. I am constantly impressed by the willingness of students to follow this route. Schools can help by liaising with banks on preferential loan rates, and by designing courses which allow a mixed mode approach and the opportunity to earn at the same time. Students may supplement their income by contributing to a school's research, consultancy and teaching activities. Such interdependency of activities and recycling of funds can help to underpin courses. For example, a realistic full cost part-time fee may generate enough resources to offer some internally funded full-time studentships.

A net benefit – the cheque is in the post!

For all the reasons noted above, I would contend that from my experience in the School of Planning, the resources cost–benefit analysis or balance sheet can be positive. But it needs some creative planning and structuring to reap economies of scale, and considerable patience. Thus initially, the cheque may be in the post, rather than your pocket!

Coordinating Inservice Education for Teachers

Diane Gaunt

Developments in the pattern of INSET courses

Until the early 1970s, very few teachers undertook courses of study beyond their initial qualifications. At that time a number of government reports gave the inservice education and training of teachers (INSET) an enormous boost as funds were made available for teachers to attend courses to update and improve their qualifications. Fundamental changes in emphasis in education during the mid-1980s were accompanied by changes in the way that INSET funds were allocated, with a shift towards narrowly focused curriculum-led staff development. The long course ceased to be the principal INSET vehicle and its place was taken by short training events run by advisory teams and consultants. Higher education has been forced to respond by making its award-bearing courses more flexible through modularization and accreditation.

The James Report 'Teacher Education and Training' recommended a great expansion in INSET for 'it is here that both the quality or our education and the standards of the profession can be most speedily, powerfully and economically improved' (DES, 1972). The Advisory Committee on the Supply and Training of Teachers (1974) put forward a 'career scenario' to illustrate the likely needs of teachers for various types of INSET at different points in their teaching lives. It referred to a teacher's own career profile and matched staff development needs to stages in the profile, but paid little attention to the needs of schools and local education authorities (LEAs). Subsequent reports added institutional, local and national needs to the list (ACSET, 1978, 1984). Thus the professional needs of individual teachers were subsumed into the needs of larger systems.

A pooling arrangement had been set up in 1955 to allow LEAs to pool some of the costs of sending teachers on long courses. As the demand for INSET rose in the post-James decade, so the pool was considered to be growing at an unacceptable rate. In 1983, DES Circular 3/83 effectively restricted secondment funded by the pool to four priority areas. Thus the freedom of choice available for teachers seeking secondment was substantially reduced. The White Paper 'Better Schools', published in March 1985, stated that the annual expenditure by LEAs on INSET stood at £100m and that these resources were not used to best advantage. A new specific grant for INSET was announced, payable to LEAs in two parts: one to cover national priority areas, the other for locally assessed priorities (DES, 1985).

At the same time as the DES was making these changes, other government departments were becoming interested in teacher education and training. In April 1985 the Manpower Services Commission invited LEAs to submit proposals for support under the Technical and Vocational Education Initiative Related Inservice Training Scheme (TRIST). It followed the Further Education Unit (1982) model of curriculum-led staff development and prepared the ground for the Local Education Authorities Training Grants Scheme (LEATGS) heralded in 'Better Schools'. Whereas previously INSET had been largely on an individual, normally voluntary, basis, LEATGS attempted to ensure that each LEA established a carefully managed framework designed to meet the needs of all teaching staff.

The Education Reform Act 1988 introduced Local Management of Schools and Colleges under which INSET monies are divided between a central fund held by the LEA and budgets delegated to schools and colleges. With substantial devolution, the role of the LEA in INSET has largely changed to that of a broker, providing activities which schools and colleges may or may not wish to buy, whilst retaining responsibility for monitoring and evaluation.

Prior to the new funding arrangements, establishments of higher education offered a comprehensive range of full-time long award-bearing courses. In 1986–87 there were 2112 full-time one-year secondments. The introduction of the LEATGS in April 1986 had a significant impact on colleges and departments of education. In 1987–88 the number of secondments fell to 673 and the following year to 439. In order to meet changing needs of teachers and to ensure their own survival, the colleges and departments had to set about changing their provision. There was a shift in mode of attendance to part-time evening courses as well a change in the design of many courses until, by the late 1980s, modular inservice schemes emerged as a predominant style (CNAA, 1990).

Modular schemes for inservice teacher education, like other modular schemes, are characterized by multiple entry and exit points with provision for entry with advanced standing on the basis of prior learning. In many cases the scheme may lead to more than one award (e.g. Certificate, Diploma, Degree), the difference being quantitative. In addition there is a move towards having differential outcomes, for example, Bachelors or Masters level from a single module, such that instead of being determined by the level of provision, the level is determined by the assessment of the outcomes. The majority of schemes adopt a single module size which is defined in terms of contact time or directed study with an indication of the total amount of private study time. Others have units of different size and use a CATS (Credit Accumulation and Transfer Scheme) rating. The degree of flexibility varies from course to course. In some modular schemes, the process of professional development which was originally embedded in a linear course has been remodelled into a modular structure through a set of prerequisites which chart a teacher's route through the course. Most schemes have a small number of compulsory modules and a large number of options. In some schemes the first module is devoted to programme planning in the belief that autonomy can be fostered through critical re-flection on professional development, leading to a negotiated programme in which coherence and progression rest with the individual teacher. Independent study modules are a feature of most schemes. The final element is normally a project or dissertation which has a synoptic function.

Modular schemes afford opportunities for partnerships between higher education establishments and LEAs. This is often achieved by the validation of LEA provision as part of a scheme. Some institutions use 'open shell' modules whereby a panel of higher education and LEA representatives approve a specific part of the LEA activity and both are involved in the assessment process. Another mechanism is to award a CATS rating to LEA courses. Individual teachers may apply for admission with advanced standing on the basis of prior certificated learning as well as experiential learning. As far as teachers are concerned, the accreditation of prior experiential learning (APEL) normally involves the assembling of evidence of professional activity which demonstrates a reflection on practice leading to identifiable learning outcomes. Some accreditation partnerships are highly developed with each teacher in the LEA being issued with a professional development portfolio which provides an acceptable format in which to record activities, reflections and action plans for school-based experience, LEA INSET and higher education INSET (DES, 1990). The accreditation of all three types of INSET provision to awards is regarded as rewarding the commitment of teachers, making INSET more attractive and helping to attract and retain a strongly motivated and well-qualified teaching force. However, improving access to award bearing INSET in this way inevitably poses questions about an erosion of standards. Triggs and Francis (1990), for example, have com-mented that not all INSET can, or should, count towards a higher quali-fication and warn that pressure to accredit all and every aspect of inservice work can only diminish the value of the awards.

The changes which have taken place in inservice education reflect a radical change in philosophy by those controlling funding. On the positive side, more staff are involved in the INSET process than was previously possible. Teachers are involved in identifying and prioritizing the INSET needs of the school or college. Some teachers are providing their own INSET, giving recognition to the qualities of the teacher as peer educator. However, the large-scale shift to school and college-focused INSET has resulted in the career development of individual teachers being increasingly neglected. The tensions between individual and institutional needs are of concern. In the short term, resources are being used to support the implementation of the Education Reform Act, especially the National Curriculum. A balance of provision is required which satisfies the demand for short, skills-based training and at the same time provides opportunities for education, the reflective scholarly activity essential for long-term professional development.

INSET provision at Oxford Polytechnic

INSET for teachers is an established part of an expanding provision of continuing professional development opportunities at Oxford Polytechnic. The award-bearing courses offered by the School of Education have been redesigned to offer greater scope for flexible and part-time study and for the recognition of other professional development activity. The modular INSET scheme now includes MA, post-graduate Diploma, BA and Certificate awards based on open and specialist programmes. It is planned to add an existing specialist qualification for teachers of the deaf to this scheme. The CertEdFE (teaching qualification for further education lecturers) is not part of the scheme but is based on a strong partnership with local colleges. All courses have been given CATS ratings. There has been substantial expansion of short course work for LEAs, consortia of individual schools, and further education colleges. Courses of two days or more in length, with associated follow-up time in the teachers' own settings, may be accredited to awards. Similar short courses mounted by other higher education providers are also recognized. LEA and school- or college-based INSET is considered for accreditation by the Employment-Based Learning Committee of the Polytechnic. Since only 50 per cent of an award can be passed on work done outside the course, open learning packages are now being produced for students who are unable to attend the Polytechnic for taught elements.

These developments, in response to changes in the INSET market, have however necessitated staff discussion and development in order to bring about fundamental shifts in attitudes and practice. Considerable debate has taken place over the levels and content of programmes and awards. Information must be disseminated about national and institutional systems of credit accumulation and transfer, including APEL, whilst moves towards collaborative partnerships with LEAs, schools and colleges, although widely supported, do require changes in traditional approaches which saw higher education institutions as sole and autonomous providers of award-bearing INSET. In turn, changes in expectations and practice need to take place amongst teachers, and their INSET organizers. Staff also have to adjust to the more complex information systems required for modular schemes, more counselling and negotiation with students and an increasing diversity of teaching modes and settings. The range and pace of innovation in education also require staff to be at the 'cutting edge' of policy implementation, particularly for short-course training, which in turn requires systematic teamwork, updating and other staff INSET within the higher education institution.

Short course work, vital for the survival of the School of Education, equally demands new skills in marketing, planning and commercial approaches to resourcing. The relationship between this new entrepreneurial work and the PCFC funded work has created dilemmas for management since the planning cycles are not synchronous. On the one hand, traditional courses have long lead times and delivery is frequently tied to an annual timetable whereas, on the other, market-driven courses frequently demand rapid responses and resources which may already be committed. Moreover, unlike some departments, the School is working with the under-funded public sector. Costings and proposals must therefore be realistic and within the limited budgets of schools, colleges and LEAs. Nevertheless, a strong profile, in priority training areas in particular, can attract considerable short- and full-cost course work, which can be further extended by the slightly more lucrative conference market.

In the uncertain climate of the early 1990s, the development, coordination and management of teacher INSET brings many new challenges. Nevertheless, institutions which can develop partnerships with schools, colleges and LEAs will be in a strong position to flourish and provide a service which responds to the professional development needs of teachers.

References

Advisory Committee on the Supply and Training of Teachers (1974) *Inservice Education and Training: some considerations.* London: DES.

Advisory Committee on the Supply and Training of Teachers (1978) *Making INSET Work.* London: DES.

Advisory Committee on the Supply and Education of Teachers (1984) *The Inservice Education, Training and Professional Development of School Teachers.* London: DES.

Council for National Academic Awards (1990) *Complex Modular Inservice Education Schemes: a Review of CNAA Provision.* London: CNAA.

Department of Education and Science (1972) *Teacher Education and Training (The James Report).* London: HMSO.

Department of Education and Science (1983) *Circular 3/83. The Inservice Teacher Training Grants Scheme.* London: DES.

Department of Education and Sciences (1984) *Circular 4/84. The Inservice Teacher Training Grants Scheme.* London: DES.

Department of Education and Sciences (1985) *Better Schools* (Cmd 9469). London: HMSO.

Department of Education and Science/HM Inspectors (1989) *The Implementation of the Local Education Authority Training Grants Scheme (LEATGS): Report on the First Year of Scheme 1987–88.* London: DES.

Department of Education and Science (1990) *News 131/90. Classrooms are for Teachers to Learn in Too.* London: DES.

Further Education Unit (1982) *Teaching Skills.* London: FEU.

Triggs, E. and Francis, H. (1990) *The Value to Education of Long (Award Bearing) Courses for Serving Teachers.* London: London University, Institute of Education.

Professional Collaboration: The Lecturer Practitioner Role

Ruth Champion

The lecturer practitioner role is central to a unique collaboration between Oxford Polytechnic and a health authority's nursing and midwifery services. This case study describes the role as it currently exists and then discusses some organizational issues, focusing in particular on issues arising from the duality of the nature of the role.

The lecturer practitioner role

Fitzgerald (1989) has defined a lecturer practitioner as 'a senior nurse who has a mastery of practice, education, management and research. Through demonstrating these collective skills s/he is able to lead a team of nurses delivering a professional service to patients, at the same time developing personal skills and knowledge in him/herself and the nurses working alongside' (p. 13). Typically, the lecturer practitioner takes on the role of ward or senior sister/charge nurse. In some areas they may be in a collegial relationship with the sister, either in one ward, within a small group of wards (subunit) or in a department where there are a number of sisters – for example, an accident and emergency department. Central to the practice element of the role, however, is authority, which not only arises from expertise but is structurally established within the ward, subunit or department. Thus lecturer practitioners must have responsibility for policies and standards in their work area, whatever the role or relationship with other staff. This authority is held to be a prerequisite for professional accountability (Hall,

1969; Rhodes, 1983; Vaughan, 1989) and underpins the policy for the development of professional nursing practice within the health authority.

Our lecturer practitioners are responsible for the practice elements of both pre-registration nursing and midwifery degrees and post-registration clinical courses. In the former, this comprises about half of the programmes (see Champion, Chapter 2). In the latter, lecturer practitioners are wholly responsible for the course organization and for approximately 80 per cent of the input. Practice-based modules, in all instances, involve the theory of practice in addition to practice itself. Lecturer practitioners, therefore, develop the modules; select and prepare mentors to work individually with students; teach the students working in their area; contribute their particular expertise to the overall teaching on the module; supervise the students' experience, validating their learning contracts; mark the students' work; and evaluate the module. Lecturer practitioners are thus professionally accountable for their educational work in addition to their clinical work. Moreover, students' learning and analyses of nursing or midwifery practice are supported by educational staff who are rooted in practice and responsible for developing both practice and education for practice. In a very real sense, lecturer practitioners are also responsible for the clinical learning environment – a term used to encompass all aspects of clinical placement which influence students' learning. This is particularly important given that research consistently points to the importance of the leadership role in influencing the pattern of quality of patient care and the quality of the learning environment (Pembrey, 1980; Fretwell, 1982; Ogier, 1982) and that research also indicates that students will practise nursing as they have experienced it during placement rather than as they have been taught it in the classroom (Hunt, 1974; Bendall, 1975; Melia, 1987).

Like their lecturer colleagues, lecturer practitioners also have students as professional tutees – a supportive role that is stable throughout the course. The professional tutor has a responsibility to facilitate, at the beginning of each term, the students' review of achievements, of developing competence and of areas of work needing attention, and overall, of ensuring that students' experience meets with statutory requirements and those of the regulating authority.

Lecturer practitioners are full members of course committees and the Health Care Studies Departmental Board and they participate in Department, Faculty and Polytechnic-wide activities. Expectations in relation to their academic and professional profile and contribution are the same as their lecturer colleagues. They are, however, employed by health authority units (e.g. hospitals, community, mental health units, etc.), their grading depending on their experience, expertise, qualifications and nature of their responsibilities. They are all, however, on senior grades equivalent to lecturers and senior lecturers in the Polytechnic – the majority on the latter. Negotiations are currently taking place to establish a grade equivalent to principal lecturer, for which the same criteria for appointment would be used as in the Polytechnic.

Within the health authority there are now approximately 50 lecturer practitioners either in post or designated (the latter being teaching staff who are clinically based and who are waiting until a vacancy or a restructuring of roles occurs that will enable them to take up their clinical responsibilities). A proportion of all lecturer practitioner salaries is paid from the education budget, the amount reflecting their proportionate input to the courses, which, in order to protect their clinical input, is never more than 50 per cent.

This description has aimed to clarify the nature of the role as it is being developed in this particular health authority–polytechnic partnership, in relation to both education and practice. The role combines the professionally accountable nursing or midwifery role of sister/charge nurse with the professionally accountable education role of lecturer. Significantly, lecturer practitioners are not seen as a 'joint appointment' although inherent to the role is dual accountability. Joint appointments typically attempt to combine two different roles in one person in order to relate the two areas of work together (Balogh and Bond, 1984; King's Fund, 1984). The role of lecturer practitioner is unified in the area of practice – the educational element arising from, and locked into, the practice role.

As a result of the creation of this role, the Polytechnic Health Care Studies Department in which the courses are based is also enmeshed in the health authority, and the courses are totally dependent on both institutions (see also Champion, Chapter 2).

Management issues

A number of issues arise from this level of institutional interdependence. Although the roles are very new – the most experienced lecturer practitioners have only been in post two-and-a-half years and have only had students in their areas for a year – four key issues have emerged to date, which can be categorized as logistical, conceptual, organizational and experiential.

Logistically, an apparently straightforward calculation (n per cent of the course input by lecturer practitioners = n per cent of the staffing resource) becomes very much more complex in its implementation. For example, the n per cent is divided between lecturer practitioners according to their contribution. However this contribution is not wholly within their control – it depends on who else is in post and ready to contribute to the course, including the readiness of the practice area in which they are working. It also depends on the numbers of students who can be adequately supervised, which in turn depends on the number and quality of nursing or midwifery staff in the work area, the nature of the clinical or community work involved and the degree to which professional patterns of practice are established. Lecturer practitioners may also choose to contribute to theoretical modules, because they have a particular expertise and because the practice modules for which they will have responsibility are not yet scheduled to run. Moreover, these factors are variable, particularly in the initial development phase. At the same time, the educational contribution to the subunit's budget needs to remain relatively constant in order to set staffing establishments.

The conceptual issues are more subtle and centre on developing an understanding of, and commitment to, the role. In practice settings, this emanates from the Director of Nursing or Midwifery services but needs to be grasped by senior nursing staff who work closely with the lecturer practitioner. Each post, for example, has at least a 50 per cent practice component, at a senior level in a subunit's structure. This is expensive unless the role encompasses the sister or senior sister role, as it adds a senior person to a team. Their 50 per cent contribution may have to be paid for by sacrificing a whole-time post at a junior grade. This clearly requires a commitment by practitioners and managers in purely economic terms.

Problems in relation to commitment to the concept of the lecturer practitioner also arise from views of nurse tutors held by practitioners and nurse managers. For example, tutors may be perceived as teaching outmoded or unrealistic theory (Bendall, 1975; Gott, 1984), raising real issues of clinical credibility. Thus tutors who take up the role have to prove their practice competence, particularly when practitioners and managers may also suspect that education is 'taking over'.

A number of organizational issues, such as funding, have already been mentioned. Staffing is also a major organizational problem. Initial opportunistic appointments were followed by the mapping of posts in each unit, using the map flexibly to review vacancies as they occurred, moving towards a stage of deliberate restructuring within subunits to create the lecturer practitioner posts. This has had to be a flexible process, taking account of vacancies, skill mix, finance, practitioners in post and available teaching staff. The final stage will be a relatively steady state with lecturer practitioners working within a subunit or between two subunits at the most (typically 2–4 wards, a department or a section in the community).

In selecting lecturer practitioners, staff from both the Polytechnic and the health authority are involved in informal visits, pre-interview discussions and the formal interview. The pattern of induction and the priorities for initial work focus are dictated by the developmental needs of the practice area, the experience of the person appointed and educational priorities. The policy is for lecturer practitioners to be in post for at least six months prior to student placement. Initial appointees had longer than this, the benefits of this being very clear from the practice development that ensured. Some appointees have had to take students within weeks of arriving, with little time to assess their practice area or prepare their own mentors. This results in huge anxiety but very rapid learning. Such precipitate appointments however clearly reduce the attention that can be given to important practice development, the major resource for which is staff development.

Experiential issues can be categorized into three main areas. The first is heavy workload. This is not surprising given the nature of the role and is a major feature of joint appointments (Balogh and Bond, op. cit.; King's Fund, op. cit.). It is essential that work demands are put in order of priority and that the work pattern established in the practice area reflects current thinking regarding professional practice, namely that team leaders or primary nurses have proper authority to exercise their professional judgement in managing patient or client care. Delegation is therefore crucial. The traditional role of ward sister – as one who is the pivot and key to all ward activity and decisions – is not tenable with the lecturer practitioner role. The emerging role of the ward sister is that of clinical leader, policy formulator, evaluator of practice and resource manager (the last being increasingly central as a consequence of current NHS reforms).

Apart from the workload generated from the combined nature of the role, additional pressure is inevitable due to the demand for practice, staff and course development, particularly since the courses are so new. All the preparation related to courses is new work and the nature of the degree programmes means that little can be 'borrowed' from already prepared materials. This new work also includes preparation of mentors, implementing contract learning and developmental work on competency measurement (see Murphy and Reading, Chapter 3). Most lecturer practitioners are also in a phase of rapid personal development themselves, which may include taking teaching qualifications, first degrees or higher degrees alongside developing the new roles. Managing the workload is therefore a major feature of any lecturer practitioner's experience.

The second experiential aspect of the role concerns belonging to two institutions, or 'living in two worlds', each of which require lecturer practitioners to be credible. This mirrors the issues that have faced nursing students for decades and in particular undergraduate nursing students (Bendall, 1975; House, 1975; Thomas, 1979; Owen, 1984; Melia, 1987; Pyne, 1988). However, the credibility of the course is very dependent on the lecturer practitioners absorbing both realities or bringing some unity to the 'two worlds', even when established practice innovation can support educational innovation.

The third experiential issue is that of role identity. It would be unusual in any organization to find 50 people occupying an established role defining their work in the same way. With the development of the new role of lecturer practitioner, there are considerable differences between the postholders in relation to perceptions of core purposes and priorities. Given the variety of role relationships that can exist with the post, this is perhaps not surprising. It contributes to the role ambiguity experienced by some of the lecturer practitioners, particularly those who have not been proactive in their thinking about professional education issues.

Role clarification is thus a fundamental aspect of establishing the role within the nursing or midwifery and the educational systems. All the postholders have had to put considerable effort into educating their nursing or midwifery peers within their subunit and unit, and their medical colleagues. In addition the relationship between lecturers and lecturer practitioners is also evolving and potential tensions erupt from time to time, usually over issues of 'ownership'. The lecturer practitioners' forum established within the Department is an important source of support and debate in this area, and also contributes to the role review being undertaken in the light of the range of issues outlined above.

Conclusion

What then has been achieved in relation to professional education by establishing the lecturer practitioner role? Although it is too early to form firm conclusions, the role undoubtedly roots learning about professional practice in practice itself (Benner, 1984; Schön, 1987). Initial impressions indicate the potential power of the role, in that lecturers no longer have to negotiate 'clinical teaching' of students – clinical supervision within an analytic and supportive framework is the proper responsibility of the lecturer practitioners who are part of the nursing or midwifery workforce. Developing work on learning contracts and competency assessment is led by those who are enmeshed in their use. Education has become a fundamental responsibility of practitioners, with very positive consequences for student learning.

In the Polytechnic, the role has had a fundamental influence on department and course development. It has institutionalized the centrality of practice to all aspects of life in the department and reduces the feeling of 'them and us' that can pervade professional course meetings where 'them' represents practitioners and 'us' academic staff.

There is a very real sense of the two perspectives – practice and education – contributing to each other's development. However it is unlikely that this would have taken place without a fundamental belief, in the Polytechnic as a whole, in the academic value of practice experience and analysis. The lecturer practitioners contribute to the growing body of staff in the Polytechnic who identify themselves as being concerned with professional education. The potential of their contribution is powerful – they are educators who are managers of practice as well as supervisors of students. They speak with authority on issues surrounding practice supervision, learning and assessment. Lecturer practitioners can act as an academic from the Polytechnic perspective and an employer from the health authority perspective. This unification focuses attention on the analytic quality of practice work and brings practice issues directly into the Polytechnic arena without the need for an intermediary. This directness of approach is perhaps the main potential of the contribution of the role to the Polytechnic.

In outlining the role of the lecturer practitioner as it has developed within a health authority – polytechnic partnership, and discussing some of the emerging issues, this case study has attempted to portray the potential of 'cross'-institutional roles in establishing professional education firmly within professional practice. Such roles have the potential to fundamentally shape both educational programmes and professional practice.

References

Balogh, R. and Bond, S. (1984) 'An analytical study of a joint clinical teaching/ service appointment on a hospital ward'. *International Journal of Nursing Studies*, **21**(2), 81–91.

Bendall, E. (1975) *So, You Passed Nurse.* London: Royal College of Nursing.

Benner, P. (1984) *From Novice to Expert: Excellence and Power in Clinical Nursing Practice.* Menlo Park, California: Addison-Wesley.

Department of Health (1989) *Working for Patients.* London: HMSO.

Fitzgerald, M. (1989) Lecturer-Practitioner: Action Researcher. MA Thesis, University of Wales, School of Nursing.

Fretwell, J. (1982) *Ward Teaching and Learning: Sister and the Learning Environment.* London: Royal College of Nursing.

Gott, M. (1984) *Learning Nursing.* London: Royal College of Nursing.

Hall, R.H. (1969) *Occupations and the Social Structure.* Englewood Cliffs, New Jersey: Prentice-Hall.

House, V. (1975) 'Paradoxes and the undergraduate student nurse'. *International Journal of Nursing Studies*, **12**, 81–6.

Hunt, J.M. (1974) *The Teaching and Practice of Surgical Dressings in Three Hospitals.* London: Royal College of Nursing.

King's Fund (1984) *Joint Clinical-Teaching Appointments in Nursing.* London: King's Fund.

Melia, K. (1987) *Learning and Working – The Occupational Socialisation of Nurses.* London: Tavistock.

Ogier, M.E. (1982) *An Ideal Sister? A study of the Leadership Style and Verbal Interactions of Ward Sisters with Nurse Learners in General Hospitals.* London: Royal College of Nursing.

Owen, G. (1984) *The Development of Degree Courses in Nursing Education – in Historical and Professional Context.* Polytechnic of the South Bank, Occasional Paper 4.

Pembrey, S. (1980) *The Ward Sister – Key to Nursing.* London: Royal College of Nursing.

Pyne, R. (1988) 'On being accountable'. *Health Visitor*, **61**, 173–5.

Rhodes, B. (1983) 'Accountability in nursing: Alternative perspectives'. *Nursing Times*, **79**(36), 65–6.

Schön, D.A. (1987) *Educating the Reflective Practitioner.* London: Jossey-Bass.

Thomas, M.C. (1979) 'Achievement and conflict in undergraduate nurses'. *Nursing Times*, Occasional Paper 75, **23**, 93–5.

Vaughan, B. (1989) 'Autonomy and accountability'. *Nursing Times*, **85**(3), 54–5.

Information Needs and Systems

Stuart Brown

For more than a decade a computer-based student management system has played a vital part in supporting the management and administration of the Modular Course at Oxford Polytechnic. During this period the nature of higher education has obviously changed and this book is concerned with

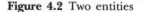

Figure 4.2 Two entities

part of that change. However, the methods and technology used to develop information systems have also evolved considerably. Methods come first, for it is now clear that the power of modern information technology is easily misapplied, frequently at considerable cost.

It is generally recognized within the Polytechnic that the current student management system must change to meet new developments such as those in professional education. From an information systems perspective, the key is the method used to analyse the requirement and control subsequent changes. The method currently used is often known as information engineering. Some indication of the way this works and the issues it raises will be evident from what follows.

What is a course?

Figure 4.2 shows two entities – an entity is any 'thing' of significance. These two entities are certainly significant. The idea of a *course* seems fundamental to teaching but all courses are made up of constituent 'things'. The term 'module' has a specific meaning at Oxford Polytechnic and so the term *unit* is preferred; modules are a type of unit.

But how are units combined into courses? Figure 4.3 suggests that the relationship involves another entity – a *course structure rule*. It also postulates that each unit may be subject to one or more *course structure rules* and that each course structure rule must be applicable to one and only one course. So a course may be composed of rules by which means its constituent units

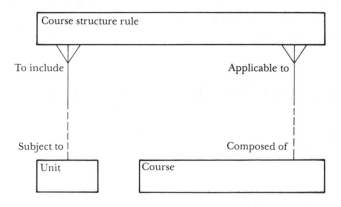

Figure 4.3 Units combined into courses – course structure rule

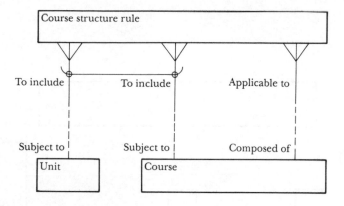

Figure 4.4 Courses within courses

are included, but also a unit may be subject to one or more rules and in this way become a component of more than one course.

This is a rigorous definition of the familiar observation that there is a 'many to many' relationship between units and courses. The prominence given to the rules associating the two is possibly less familiar. The creation of these rules must be authorized – they must be academically valid, but must also be standardized across the institution and probably with automated support if the construction of courses is to be flexible and responsive.

Courses within courses

Courses are composed, not only of units but may include other courses. In fact, it may not be clear which course a student is taking until an award is made. A one-year post-graduate diploma may lead to a two-year MSc. It all depends at which point the student decides to stop. Figure 4.4 defines this situation. It says that a rule may include a unit within a course or another course within a course. Obviously the units which make up the 'subordinate' course will also be included in the 'super course'.

A correct organizational response to the maintenance of course structure rules may be important to the rationalization of the relationships between the many units and courses on offer, but it is likely to prove vital to the success of any computer system supporting the type of learning environment discussed in this book.

Resources, timetabling and events

Figure 4.5 extends the entity model in several directions. It suggests that each unit may be comprised of one or more *events*. By event, we mean

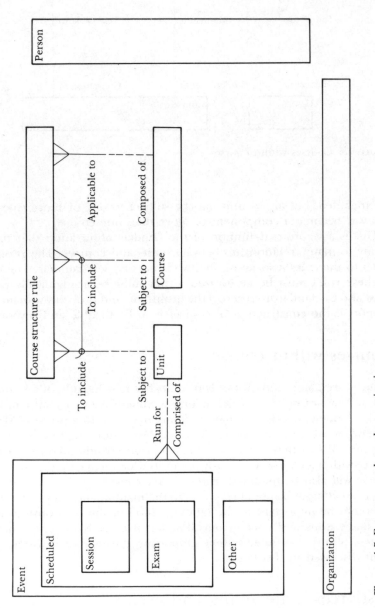

Figure 4.5 Events, people and organizations

scheduled events such as a teaching session or examination, which must be timetabled in some way or possibly other events or activities which are significant components of the unit. The model also says that each event must be run for one and only one unit and also that events are not related directly to courses, but always run for units. This may be incorrect, but it is important that a correct model is agreed because we are here dealing with the basis of any resource allocation (e.g. timetabling) and accounting algorithms; it is the level of the event that physical and human resources are used.

Are students people?

Following this thread of resource management, Figure 4.5 hints at two important entities which we have not considered so far – *person* and *organization*. Detailed relationships are not shown, but this does not prevent a general discussion.

All of the entities that we have considered (event, unit, course structure rule) are related to people (person). By person we could mean a member of the Polytechnic staff, in which case a person might lead or supervise an event; a person may be responsible for a unit or a course and a person may authorize a rule allowing a unit to be included in a course. If we are to have a robust systematic approach to (for instance) scheduling and keeping track of staff or the authorization, validation and management of courses and units we need to be clear about these relationships.

What is meant by organization? Within the Polytechnic this refers to the schools, departments and sections which make up the institution, but we also deal in a complex manner with other external organizations, which have the same basic attributes (e.g. addresses) and structures (e.g. departmental). How are these related to the other entities on the model? Are courses related to departments? Are courses related to external organizations? In the case of professional education this seems very likely. What about the location, resourcing, cost and charging for events?

The relationship between person and organization is interesting. In the simple case of a member of staff, that person is probably associated with one or more departments or sections. However, some of the teaching expertise, especially in professional education, may well come from outside the Polytechnic – from other organizations.

The external organization will be providing a service to our own (possibly at a cost), but this immediately opens up the prospect of the Polytechnic providing services for that external organization – we have a point of contact. Of course, a very similar relationship exists with students, especially those involved in professional education. They come from other organizations and are in a sense contacts. This type of information is important to marketing. If we are to develop any comprehensive information resource in this respect, we must put in place systems which capture this data and make it available for constructive use.

Of course, the same person might be a student on one course, an external lecturer on another and for the other half of the week teach as an employee of the Polytechnic! In such a case the person would be a customer, external resource, internal resource and contact. This suggests that the familiar distinction between students and employees or other people must be questioned. It is probable that we need systems capable of maintaining a more complex and integrated view.

Who owns this model?

This short discussion of an incomplete information model cannot do justice to the techniques involved. However, the purpose is not to explain the method, but to raise the question of the contribution that the method can make to the successful development of the Polytechnic, and professional education in particular.

At a simple technical level, the models define the structure of the database upon which any computer system will depend. If the model is wrong the system is unlikely to work satisfactorily. It may be a serious and expensive matter for the management and administration of the institution if things do go wrong at the design stage. However, the educational impact would be more subtle, appearing in the form of restrictions and inflexibility in 'the computer system', more paperwork to make up for deficiencies in the system model and more general inconvenience.

This situation may be familiar; computer systems rarely fit fully and elegantly into the organization that they are supposed to assist. This is why the information engineering techniques hinted at above have developed the way that they have. They are based on the view that *the system* is not 'the thing in the computer', but a description of the organization and its constituent processes, some of which may be automated.

So information engineering starts by producing a concise manageable model of information and functions (not considered in this account) required and operating within the organization. But what then? It is important that these models are judged, amended and used by the appropriate people. Often this is the senior management, but in the case of an academic institution and models of educational activities, a wide range of legitimate interests may be involved.

In Oxford Polytechnic it is as yet too early to answer the fundamental question of who owns the information model. It is not the information systems practitioner, to whom the model is only of use if it reflects the way that those who control the organization want it to work. However, with a number of committees and individuals influencing events, responsibility for the model and control of the changes impacting it remains problematical.

Openness?

The strategic business analysis skills required in the early stages of the information engineering method and for the production of the information model are frequently bought in from consultancy organizations at considerable cost. However, the models are even more valuable in the sense that they include information on the way that an organization is approaching complex questions which may be vital to competitive advantage. Consequently they and the information strategy of which they form a part are generally considered confidential to the company.

If a competitive ethos also applies within higher education, should institutions not guard their information models similarly? Surely the blueprint for a flexible innovative system of professional education would provide competitive edge? To some degree, the answer to these questions must be yes. However, an isolationist approach seems to conflict with the idea of Credit Accumulation and Transfer Schemes as well as attempts to increase the ability of students to choose and move between institutions, a line of development which is important to professional education initiatives. Furthermore, the national and possibly international dimension to higher education requires the exchange of information in relation to funding and comparative quality.

To the extent that ideas such as course, unit, assessment and credit are common across institutions and funding bodies, it seems sensible to share models and possibly agree common public domain models to assist in the efficient, accurate and systematic interchange of information. Such a statement and much else in this account, is likely to be mistaken as a proposal for systematic rigidity and restrictiveness, when it does, in fact, propose no more than effective communication and control of change.

A note on the method

A useful discussion of information engineering and related issues is provided by Martin (1984).

The diagramming conventions used in this account are those advocated by CASE*Method, a proprietary version of information engineering developed by the Oracle Corporation. A good introduction to the diagrams is provided by Barker (1990).

The diagrams used in this account are not definitively correct, but have been adapted to support the points discussed.

References

Barker, R. (1990) *CASE*Method Entity Relationship Modelling.* London: Addison-Wesley.
Martin, J. (1984) *An Information Systems Manifesto.* New York: Prentice-Hall.

5

Interprofessionalism

Hazel Bines

Interprofessionalism is an important element of professional practice, which can do much to ensure the quality and effectiveness of professional services. Its desirability is clear, in terms of the needs, rights and expectations of clients, the range of expertise required in particular tasks or services and the reduction of conflict and frustration for professionals themselves. However little systematic attention has been given to the development of interprofessional working, through policy, practice, research or professional education.[1]

There are a number of reasons for this. First, interprofessionalism is not easy to define. It is often seen as both inter- and multi-disciplinary in nature, with a range of consequent approaches to practice. Secondly, the increasing complexity of professional concerns, expertise, activities and services has tended to result in greater specialization and finer divisions of labour, rather than generic or collaborative models and approaches. Thirdly, being a member of a particular profession involves commitment to certain values, identity, expertise and interests. There is therefore considerable potential for conflict and territoriality, especially since the history and development of the professions has largely been based on securing status through exclusive knowledge and occupational demarcation.

Despite the acknowledged consequences, interprofessionalism remains a rhetorical goal which is rarely fully implemented. Attempts to change attitudes and practice, such as the development of teamwork, have not resulted in fundamental change. Indeed, as Dingwall has noted, 'talking about teamwork is largely a way of making certain sorts of occupational claim rather than a way of concerting action' (1982, p. 99). Interprofessionalism is thus a crucial aspect of the debate on professional education.

Developing interprofessionalism

Although it is not possible in this book to explore in detail the debate about inter- and multi-disciplinary/professional approaches, the variety of ways in which such terms are used necessitates some operational definitions. This chapter is primarily concerned with integration and synthesis as the essential characteristic of interdisciplinary work, rather than with the additive, aggregated or juxtapositional nature of multidisciplinary or multiprofessional approaches (Gyamarti, 1986). Interdisciplinarity is regarded as being primarily concerned with knowledge, including both epistemological and social aspects, while interprofessionalism is concerned with the social division of labour and social organization of professions, and in particular the collaboration of different professions in providing services for clients, solving a particular problem or set of problems or executing one or more tasks.

Interdisciplinary work thus involves the analytical incorporation of more than one discipline or area of professional knowledge, the use of one discipline to consider another and above all not defining phenomena or problems through the exclusive perspective of one discipline. Interprofessional work involves taking an holistic view of the needs of a client, problem or task and not defining or acting within a situation from one particular professional slant. It may comprise work across major professional boundaries and services (for example, planning and engineering in the built environment), or interprofessionalism within a particular service (for example, between the range of specialist professionals in the health service). In turn, both interdisciplinary and interprofessional work have reciprocal and synthesizing implications for each other.

Effective interdisciplinary or interprofessional work is based on the recognition that, paradoxically, progress in knowledge and service provision has led to the very fragmentation which can obstruct our capacity to understand or do something about the phenomena which specialization was intended to address (Gyamarti, ibid.). Conditions for the development of interprofessionalism within professional education therefore include the acknowledgement of such problems as an intrinsic element of professionalism, and the recognition that many areas of professional work are too complex to be solved by one discipline or profession.

However this may lead to major tensions in the aims and purposes of professional education. Effective education for a particular profession, under current patterns of professionalism, requires the learning of specialized expertise as well as socialization into a particular professional role, to foster depth of knowledge and experience, identity and commitment. Interprofessionalism however, requires such knowledge and identity to be deconstructed and recast in new frameworks and forms of knowledge and action. Developing an interprofessional perspective, and the knowledge and experience to make it work in practice, may thus make potentially conflicting, or at least, confusing, demands on both students and teachers. There is thus a strong argument for postponing interprofessional work to continuing professional development (CPD) courses, when basic expertise and practice has been mastered. However, such courses may then have to unpack the insular attitudes and practices developed in initial training and subsequent experience. Moreover, the new professional then remains entirely unprepared for the interprofessional communication and collaboration required in his or her future working life. Whatever the difficulties, interprofessionalism ought ideally to be a significant element of all professional courses, both initial and CPD.

However, the development of an interprofessional approach or element in courses has been somewhat neglected to date. In addition to the reasons outlined above, professional courses, and related organization for course development, accreditation and funding, tend to reflect the discrete organization of professions in practice. Professional education has also developed its own standing on claims that highly specialized knowledge and training are required. Although the teaching of contributory academic disciplines has often been multidisciplinary or interdisciplinary in nature, very little attention has been given to the need for, or skills involved in, interprofessional collaboration. However the new focus on professional competence, problem-solving and the practice context is fostering a greater interest in interprofessional work, since this reflects the experience which students actually encounter and need. Courses have also been influenced by external criticism of the lack of interprofessional cooperation and its consequences for clients and other aspects of professional activity. Nevertheless, knowledge, skills and experience of interprofessional working still need to become a much more explicit and central aspect of professional competence[2] and the desire for cooperation across the boundaries of education for different professions has as yet to be fully translated into practice.

The development of interprofessional perspectives and action includes two key, related processes. The first involves analysis of the professional 'self', that is the particular professional values, identities, expertise and ways of working involved in one's own profession. The second involves developing an understanding of the professional perspectives and actions of others, through communicating and sharing these, together with experience of interprofessional work. Education for interprofessionalism is thus another form of professional socialization, though this time it is based in a complex interrelationship and synthesis of 'self' and 'other' into what 'we' might do , together.

There are a number of ways in which this can be approached. Most frequently, interprofessional development is based on substantive areas of knowledge and/or activity common to two or more professions, such as working with families, providing a particular health care service or design for the built environment. It can also be developed through a focus on the generic skills and activities common to many professions, even though these may be exercised in different contexts. These include:

- common skills related to clients – for example, interpersonal skills, needs assessment, communication skills
- common skills related to resource allocation and management – for example, matching available services to client needs, planning time or other resource allocation, evaluating the effectiveness of a particular intervention

- general management skills – for example, developing teamwork or managing changes in service delivery.

However, although elaborating such commonality can be very valuable, there is always the danger that it will primarily be conceived in aggregated or multiprofessional terms alone. This may not overcome problems of territoriality or develop the synthesis of truly interprofessional work. The development of interprofessionalism also requires dialectic contrast and differentiation, in order to engender a reframing and synthesis of perspectives and problems. It is here that the methodology of interdisciplinary work can be particularly useful. The insights and the theoretical and methodological approaches of another discipline or profession can be used to identify and analyse commonalities and differences (and why they occur). This may both foster understanding of other disciplines/professions, and even more importantly, one's own. It could involve, for example, different health care professionals considering similarities and differences between their knowledge bases, approaches to service provision and to clients/patients, and ways of solving professional problems. Or it may comprise examining a particular profession from the viewpoint of a particular discipline, for example drawing on sociology to explore the assumptions and practices of social work. Such understanding can then be drawn into a new, interprofessional synthesis.

Courses also need to address the social as well as the epistemological aspects of interprofessionalism. These include the development of skills related to communication, teamwork and the management of conflict, together with understanding of the history of the professions and the constraints of current professional organization. All of these elements can then be brought together through experience, in practice, of effective approaches to interprofessional work.

Course design and delivery

The approaches considered above can be developed in a number of ways. However, course design to develop interprofessionalism typically involves either a common/generic foundation or core element, followed or paralleled by more specialist study, or the development of certain shared course elements between otherwise separate professional courses. Both approaches attempt to model interprofessional collaboration by developing interprofessional conceptions of knowledge and problems and by mixing students (and staff) together during training, so that they can develop understanding and experience of working together. A few courses may reject any form of specialization and exclusively focus on interprofessional work. Alternatively, the course may remain discrete but nevertheless include an interprofessional element. Instead of mixing with students on other professional courses, opportunities may be provided to work with other professionals at some time during the course. Teacher education students, for example, may be given opportunities to shadow an educational psychologist or an education social worker, and such professionals are often invited to talk about their role in schools. In addition, both integrated and discrete courses may include placements in other professional services or interprofessional settings. Teaching is likely to be based on both multidisciplinary and interdisciplinary approaches, with the balance determined by the particular aims and purpose of the course. For example, the varied aspects of health care may be considered in a multidisciplinary way within a discrete nurse education course, in order to foster understanding, from a specialized viewpoint, of the perspectives of other health care professionals. In contrast, an integrated course for a range of health care professionals, designed to develop the interprofessional dimensions of health care provision, will primarily focus on interdisciplinary and interprofessional synthesis.

The design of interprofessional elements of courses will also reflect particular aims and objectives. It is important to distinguish, for example, between developing the awareness of a particular group of students as to the role and perspectives of other professionals whom they may encounter, and the specific development of teamwork skills for interprofessional working. The former can be facilitated through meeting and discussing with other professionals during courses, whether these are practising professionals or students on other professional courses. The latter requires course units which specifically develop such skills, such as simulations of interprofessional activity, attachments to other professionals/services or practical placements in interprofessional settings.

Interprofessionalism can also be facilitated by the use of particular teaching and learning methods. Jaques has suggested that these should address the issues and problems of interprofessional working and even more importantly, model the processes involved, such as dialogue, negotiation, interaction and problem solving. Techniques may include: games and exercises; topic and case discussions; role play; peer teaching; joint project work. Problem-based learning, discussed in Chapter 4, would also seem to offer a particularly useful approach to developing interprofessionalism, bringing together different professionals to solve a common problem. The two key principles involved are firstly, the focus on group work, reflecting the nature of teams and interprofessional working in general, and secondly, the emphasis on experiential learning, to facilitate transfer of learning to new situations, further student development and ensure that learning is seen to be relevant to daily life and work (Jaques, 1986). The importance of experience, as the most powerful of learning tools, should also be reflected in course design and delivery. Although particular units or short courses with an interprofessional focus may have some influence on the beginning or experienced professional, sharing perspectives and taking part in group activities may not be enough. There is a need for more extended field placements to demonstrate and develop both the value of, and the techniques and processes involved in, interprofessional work.

In addition, as a number of commentators have argued, professional education in itself is unlikely to have a major impact on the development of interprofessionalism until service delivery and working practices change in the student's future or current employment. It is also unlikely that effective interprofessional education will be developed until better interprofessional collaboration takes place within professional education itself. This last aspect of interprofessionalism has been somewhat neglected, despite its importance, and will now be discussed.

Interprofessionalism within professional education

There are two major dimensions of interprofessionalism within professional education. First, there is the cooperation required to develop professional education within each professional community, in particular the relationships between educators, students, employers, other working professionals and professional bodies. This nexus of sponsors, providers and clients, as discussed in Chapter 1, involves complex and often differing views about standards of entry to and exit from courses, content and modes of study, demand and supply (of both labour and courses), and control and accountability. Even though those involved may be members of one particular profession, their different positions, responsibilities and expertise may generate differences of perspective as great as those between members of different professions. However such issues are rarely seen as part of the debate about interprofessionalism. If they can be viewed in this way, some of the approaches to developing effective interprofessionalism could be applied to such relationships, with positive results. For example, the identification of common and different perspectives and skills could then provide an explicit base for teamwork to design a new course, ensuring experience of collaboration in practice, facilitated by skills in communication, in the management of cooperation and conflict and other aspects of teamwork.

Similar points can be made about the second dimension of interprofessionalism within professional education, namely cooperation between professions, to enhance professional education as a whole. Currently, this is most likely to involve academics responsible for professional courses, since, as noted in Chapter 4, they tend to hold the ring in relation to interprofessionalism in professional education. However, the developing partnership of educators and others within each professional community, and the importance of interprofessionalism in practice to develop students' perspectives and skills, increasingly require other participants to be involved, such as employers and professional bodies. In both instances, the task is to ensure effective partnerships and collaboration which will enhance rather than impede the development of professional education.

Partnership within the professional community

As noted in Chapter 2, control of the technocratic model of professional education was largely invested in institutions of higher education. Although professional bodies might control accreditation, higher education staff retained considerable autonomy in relation to the design and delivery of courses. Employers and other working professionals enjoyed little influence or participation in course delivery, even in relation to the practicum.

However, the post-technocratic model assumes a more equal relationship between educators and other members of the professional community. In addition, the development of employment-based learning, accreditation and CPD courses has resulted in a closer partnership between employers, services and higher education. The new focus on professional competence, and the increasing importance of the practicum, also require greater participation in professional education by working professionals, who in turn may also be students themselves, on CPD courses.

Interprofessional cooperation between these various participants can be developed through the partnerships which have been examined in this and previous chapters, namely the partnerships between higher education institutions, employers, other professionals, professional bodies and the students themselves. The case studies in this and other chapters indicate some of the ways in which such partnerships can be successfully developed. In particular, as noted by Clare Gillies (below), the post-technocratic model of professional education, in focusing on professional competence for operational practice, would seem to offer a starting point for course design to which all participants can contribute. The joint development of courses, between a higher education institution and a service (Champion, Chapter 2; Gillies and Harris, below), new requirements for the practicum (Glenny and Hickling, Chapter 2), the joint assessment of competence (Murphy and Reading, Chapter 3) and the appointment of lecturer practitioners (Champion, Chapter 4) all presume a greater involvement of employers and other working professionals in pre-service professional education. In turn, the accreditation of employment-based learning (Robertson, Chapter 2), the customization of distance learning (Hughes, Chapter 3) and other developments in CPD courses (McDougall, Chapter 2; Gaunt, Chapter 4) should similarly enhance such partnerships. Nevertheless, as all these case studies demonstrate, such cooperation does require time, together with the effective resolution of differing perspectives and interests.

Developing professional education

In turn, the development of professional education as a whole requires careful consideration of the relationships between the various participants involved, in order to develop more effective partnerships. Issues include: the relationship between teachers of the professional element of courses and teachers of contributory academic disciplines; cooperation across and beyond the higher education institution between those involved in education for different professions; the role and status of professional education within higher education; and the relationship of the higher education institution to the professional and other groups involved in professional courses.

In our experience at least, the most straightforward of these would seem to be the development of greater cooperation between those involved in education for different professions within an institution. Although territoriality is inevitably present, its intensity is more easily reduced in an educational setting, particularly when there are demonstrable benefits from collaboration, including the sharing of approaches to course design and delivery and of solutions to common problems. As noted in Chapter 1, and elsewhere, Oxford Polytechnic staff now regularly contribute to the design, development, validation and review of each others' courses and there are a number of joint ventures. These developments have been further encouraged by an interprofessional group and by regular seminars and conferences on professional education, as well as by a growing consensus over the need to implement the post-technocratic model of professional education, whatever the particular profession involved.

Nevertheless, such developments do depend on explicit recognition of the issues which colleagues do have in common and the factors which are most likely to bring them together. These include: curriculum frameworks; common knowledge areas; teaching, learning and assessment methods; staff development needs; resource needs; and opportunities for professional and social interaction. In relation to curriculum frameworks, our Modular Course, and the general move toward unit or module-based design for other courses, provide structures which can easily facilitate the sharing and/or cross-accreditation of units between courses as well as the sharing of staff. The identification of common knowledge areas has been slightly more problematic, in that an area like human physiology or social policy, although common to many professional courses, may have a particular professional slant, thus restricting rather than expanding the potential for sharing a knowledge base. Nevertheless, many courses do draw on common modules or units. There is also a growing recognition that much can be gained from sharing teaching and learning methods common to many professional courses, such as the use of the practicum or problem-based learning, and from sharing common problems, such as the assessment of professional competence. Common staff development and resource needs include the support of students in the practicum, professional updating and the preservation of specialized teaching accommodation. The provision of formal and informal opportunities to share such issues, which are meaningful to all professional courses, is one way of overcoming what seem to be the major blockages to such cooperative development, namely historical isolation, not realizing the commonality of issues, lack of time to meet other colleagues and pressures of work on one's own courses.

Such cooperation may also be successful because it does not, as yet, impinge to any great degree on the autonomy of particular professional courses. Ideas may be shared but there is no direct pressure from one course on another to change its practice. In contrast, the interprofessional relationship between teachers of the professional element of courses and teachers of contributory academic disciplines can be more problematic, since both are involved in teaching a particular course. Moreover, the trend in the post-technocratic model of professional education away from 'pure' teaching of the cognate discipline(s) towards contextualization in issues of practice, has a number of implications for the relationship between discipline-based and profession-based staff. As noted in Chapters 2 and 3, this may well undermine the discipline, leading to potential conflict over course content, teaching methods or assessment, especially when profession-based staff retain a strong loyalty to their particular professional culture and discipline-based staff maintain traditional conceptions of, and approaches to teaching, their subject. Inevitably, as noted by George (below), social issues of status, resources and power are also an important element of such relationships.

Nevertheless, such problems can be overcome, particularly since the integration of contributory academic disciplines within profession-based course units is likely to require team teaching, or at least, cooperative course development and review. However, such teamwork does have to model the principles of interdisciplinary or interprofessional work in general, if it is to be successful. It is important, for example, to make explicit the ways in which differences of content or methodology between disciplines and professions may affect teaching approaches so that different student and staff expectations and experiences can be managed in a systematic way (see also Champion, Chapter 2). The staffing of course units, to deliberately bring together discipline-based and profession-based staff into a teaching team, can also provide practical experience of the benefits of such teamwork, which may increase effective cooperation. On our new occupational therapy degree, for example, modules concerned with the anatomical and physiological aspects of occupational therapy are taught collaboratively by a life scientist and two occupational therapists, a pattern which is likely to be continued in proposals for physiotherapy and radiotherapy courses and which is increasingly being adopted for the teaching of other disciplines in other professional courses.

Issues surrounding the relationship between profession and discipline-based staff, and between educators for different professions, reflect the general role and position of professional education in higher education, which has, until recently, frequently been marginal. They also reflect the low priority given in higher education to teaching and to interdisciplinary work (Becher, 1989). However, the increasing confidence of educators for the professions in the rigour of professional education *per se*, together with their involvement in many innovative developments, such as new modes of study, and partnerships with employers, is beginning to change both the status and the credibility of professional education within higher education. Nevertheless, explicit institutional policies and planning remain important, to both develop a culture of interprofessional cooperation amongst those involved in professional education and to support the continued growth and effectiveness of professional education within higher education as a whole.

Such policies and planning are also required to ensure the continuing partnership within particular professional communities between higher education, employers, other working professionals and professional bodies. In addition, as noted by Dufton (below), positive attitudes towards inter-professional collaboration still need to be developed in the field, even in closely related services. Institutions may be able to play a role in bringing different professional communities together to develop common models of professional education, share effective approaches to teaching, learning and assessment and above all, sponsor a greater degree of interprofessional development within and across courses for different professions. The community role espoused by many institutions could also be developed to encompass an aspect of professional education which has rarely been considered to date, namely the involvement of the consumers or clients of professional services in the education of current and future professionals. Such an involvement would not only offset some of the criticisms of professional attitudes and power relationships in relation to clients and consumers but could also help to ensure that professional formation does address the changing nature of professions in society as a whole.

Conclusion

A major theme of this book has been the many common issues involved in education for the professions, ranging from issues of course design and delivery to those of management and partnership. Although, as noted in Chapter 1, heterogeneity is a significant element of professionalism, there are many common elements in professional knowledge, action and problems which are reflected, even in quite apparently disparate professions, in similar approaches to professional formation. The historical development of professions, and of professional education, has been based on increasingly specialized divisions of expertise and labour, between educators and practitioners and between the different professions.

Nevertheless, as the case studies below illustrate, it is possible to develop interdisciplinary and interprofessional approaches to professional education which can begin to break down such divisions, in a range of professions. Anne Dufton considers the issues involved for paramedical professions and John Glasson, the successful development of interdisciplinarity for the built environment. Interprofessional collaboration between employers and educators is considered by Clare Gillies and Peter Harris. Finally, Peter George discusses the implications for academic disciplines of the different models of professional education and the relationship between discipline-based and profession-based staff within an institution.

The recasting of partnerships within professional communities, to support professional education, does demonstrate the possibility, and the potential, of such change. The development of collaboration between professions, in the interests of clients and services, is more problematic, if only because more conflicting interests and boundaries are involved. Nevertheless, if the key task for the future can be identified as developing an interprofessional culture for both education and practice, the future development of professionalism may be much enhanced.

Notes

1. I would like to thank Anne Dufton, Peter George and David Jaques for their comments on previous drafts of this chapter.
2. For example, the criteria (competences) for teacher education courses identified by the Council for the Accreditation of Teacher Education (CATE) make no reference to interprofessional cooperation, nor to any aspect of teamwork in relation to the range of services for children.

References

Becher, T. (1989) *Academic Tribes and Territories.* Milton Keynes: SRHE/Open University Press.
Dingwall, R. (1982) 'Problems of teamwork in primary care'. In Clare, A.W. and Corney, R.H. (eds) *Social Work and Primary Health Care.* London: Academic Press.
Gyamarti, G. (1986) 'The teaching of the professions: an interdisciplinary approach'. *Higher Education Review,* **18**(2), 33–43.
Jaques, D. (1986) *Training for Teamwork: The Report of the Thamesmead Interdisciplinary Project.* Oxford: Oxford Polytechnic, Educational Methods Unit.

CASE STUDIES

The Paramedical Opportunity

Anne Dufton

It seems somewhat paradoxical, that in a chapter devoted to the inter-disciplinary, interprofessional approach to training, at least one group of professions should be dealt with separately. This is partly to do with the division of a complex thesis into coherent portions, but with respect to the paramedical field, also a reflection of their placing on the care-continuum.

The descriptor 'paramedical' is sometimes used for all professions allied to medicine but more precisely is used to embrace occupational therapy, physiotherapy, chiropody, dietetics, orthoptics and speech therapy. The status of the education and training of professions allied to medicines has been closely related to the status of medicine itself. The very term 'allied to medicine' evokes the conventional hierarchical relationship of doctors and other professions working in the health field.

Most of these professions share (to varying degrees) certain characteristics in common with each other and with nursing. They are professions which are traditionally perceived as:

- female dominated
- non-graduate
- vocational (in the 'committed' sense)
- low paid
- having subordinate status in the medical hierarchy.

They are also the subject of recent reports on professional practice, structure and training. They are seeking graduate status as the norm, the training period has lengthened and the demographic down-turn is likely to hit them disproportionately to many other professional groups which are less reliant on female entrants.

Some have moved more quickly than others to degree status. The 'scientific' element within the diploma course and A level entrance requirements of physiotherapy, for example, were more easily seen as foundations to degree development than was the more broadly based occupational therapy training with its craft element and O level entry. It is also probably true that historically the physiotherapists have seen a hierarchy in which their profession ranks higher than occupational therapy but the current perspectives reflect a new view of professionalism (*Physiotherapy*, 1988). But there is still some way to go as the editorial writer in *Therapy Weekly* (4 October 1990) comments:

> The CSP's controversial, and ultimately inconclusive, consultation exercise on relations between the two professions in late 1988, may have left some heaving a secret sigh of relief that the 'merger debate' was out of the way for another few years.
>
> But it will not go away – not as long as overlapping roles and artificial boundaries confound efficient patient care, confuse patients and spark interprofessional animosities. To ignore this is to regard being a 'professional' too narrowly.

It can reasonably be argued that (some) educationalists have an obsession with interdisciplinarity and interprofessionalism and that there is no virtue in joint or shared learning for its own sake – it has to be related to something, preferably to professional practice. This is an acceptable view and one which has dictated developments to date at Oxford Polytechnic.

In 1986, the National Training Forum (NTF) published a discussion paper which was intended to stimulate debate around issues of training of professions allied to medicine (PAMs). The NTF quoted a comparative review of education and training in the UK, West Germany, USA and Japan which suggested that the common characteristics of successful enterprises were (NTF, 1986, p. 4):

- effective use of knowledge and skills in changing circumstances
- performance of multi-task operations
- crossing occupational boundaries and working in multi-occupational teams
- explorations of gaps in knowledge skills needed when faced with unfamiliar situations.

At the time of its publication the NTF views were regarded by many practitioners as ill-formed and far too radical. NTF anticipated this reaction when they indicated that their proposals for joint learning would not happen because professional bodies 'police the occupational boundaries', boundaries which developed historically but were no longer relevant within current practice.

This use of the term *boundaries* is interesting in that it typifies the conventional approach to professional training which rightly, focuses upon establishing professional identity, but in doing so has stressed the exclusivity of practice and failed to engender the concept of team-based working. In fact, while it is possible to identify discrete knowledge areas and/or levels of knowledge, it is very difficult to distil out skills *unique* to the training and experience of these professional groups. For example, paramedics with a training which falls far short of that given to doctors, carry out medical functions in the developing world. Practice nurses have shown that they can work along the boundaries of medical/nursing care. Few perhaps would go as far as the NTF in their view that (ibid., p. 5):

> The present multiple cultures of the NHS encourage a view of training and trainers which is unprofessional and fragmented. The need is to develop a new approach with much less emphasis on professional boundaries, which is more task-orientated and competency-based.

Tasks, skills and competences are increasingly central to professional education. They are also central to NCVQ philosophy, and there are those who believe that as the NCVQ develops competences at levels above 5, the specialisms argument which underlies the current professional training will be breached.

Professional development

An important consequence of the up-grading of professional training has been the reflection brought to bear upon practice by actual practitioners. Thus it is nurses who are looking at nursing roles, occupational therapists and physiotherapists who are investigating alternative applications, not doctors and not academics. In the areas of practice covered by the PAMs, research has shown the value of new approaches and new techniques, and all these professions have been asked to take on more specialist roles at a time when there are pressures to blur the professional boundaries. This is coming to fruition at a time when political pressures are acute and when there is more media attention than ever before on the delivery of health care services. Change is being called for both from within the profession (new methods of treatment) and from without the profession as the 'clients' become more sophisticated and articulate (consumer groups, patient consultative groups). Change is the order of the day (ENB, 1985, p. 1):

> The health care needs and expectations of society change over time and the role of the professional carer changes and develops to meet these needs and demands. Professional training and education courses cannot remain static and those responsible for approving institutions to provide courses must be sensitive and responsive to changing reality. At the present time, the strategic plans for health care being developed by Health Authorities will reflect these needs and must be matched by strategic proposals for education and training courses.

Implications for training

According to Raikes and Simpkiss (1986, p. 6).

> Inter-departmental and interdisciplinary trust does not take place overnight and constant hard work is required to change outmoded and rigid concepts. Increasing specialisation must not lead to fragmentation and failure to recognise the needs of the whole child through underestimation of colleagues' expertise and knowledge of latest developments.

One of the most important implications for the development of these professions is that the nature of training and the Educational environment in which it takes place must be designed to build in interprofessional contacts and awareness. However, one of the problems is that we are not sure yet – as educators – how to effect this. As has already been suggested, the necessary development of professional identity and professional integrity may also be the means of building up barriers to interprofessional awareness and co-operation. (There are examples of related professional courses taking place on adjacent floors in the same building with no contact between staff or students.) An interesting project in Thamesmead concluded (Jaques, 1986, p. 69):

> There is little doubt that the separateness of training in health visiting, medicine and social work respectively, reinforced by their distinctive

approaches to training and practice, seems to contribute to difficulties in crossing professional boundaries.

The modular course structure at Oxford Polytechnic provides a framework for interprofessional learning. Students pursuing particular professional qualifications are not locked into closed (one-outlet) courses. But sharing parts of courses will not of itself bring about shared learning or interprofessional awareness. The real challenge for the course designers is to provide fieldwork/clinical placements which demonstrate the value of, and the techniques needed for, team-based interprofessional working.

There is evidence from the experience of teacher-training, that new approaches to teaching inculcated during the training period can founder if the newly qualified teacher finds him/herself in the first appointment in a very traditional setting (Lacey, 1977). Any new approaches to practice may only be successful where there is a partnership between trainers, employers and practitioners. This realization is particularly important for inservice training. The development of new approaches through initial training is ideally preceded by, but minimally and critically developed in parallel with, inservice schemes designed through the key-triangle which is discussed later in this section.

In Oxford Polytechnic, an important plank in the training strategy for health and related professions has been the development of a Degree in Health Care Studies for registered health care professionals. The course has a basic tenet, that current issues in health care should be studied in an interdisciplinary context and modules have been developed specifically to encourage students (who could of course be practising professionals in nursing, midwifery, health visiting, district nursing, physiotherapy, occupational therapy, radiography or other related professionals), to bring to the course their varied experience, knowledge and skills. The majority of students will be practitioners in the locality, and this has the additional advantage that relationships may be formed that will carry over into day to day interprofessional communication and practice, and thus provide the base for the interprofessional placements of students pursuing initial training. Occupational therapy is now offered at degree level within the Oxford Polytechnic Modular Course. It is hoped to add physiotherapy in the near future and thus provide a natural setting in which joint learning can lay the foundations for interprofessional practice, reinforced by clinical and community placements where practitioners share the underlying philosophy which has informed training.

The next decade

As a number of statutory changes in health and social services highlight changing patterns of delivery, there is a new emphasis on community care and cross-professional management. A Department of Health Training Strategy Group suggests that amongst the main staff and professional groups affected by changes in community care are nurses, physiotherapists, psychologists, occupational therapists, managers, general practitioners and finance and information management staff. They look to (Department of Health, 1990, para 1.5):

> training solutions which will support specific NHS roles with a view to maximising at every opportunity the prospect of that training happening on a shared basis with staff from other agencies.

The Children Act (1989), similarly calls for much closer co-operation between health and social services.

Client needs rarely divide up neatly into separate medical, social, educational needs.[1] The failure of effecting this interrelationship/interdependence has been illustrated by the tragic child abuse cases which become the focus of media attention. As *The Guardian* (4 December 1985) reported on Jasmine Beckford's death:

> It is still the inescapable fact that not just they (social workers) but most of the main actors contributed to the tragedy – social services personnel, medical staff, health visitors and their managers, schools and magistrates – some more than others.

The need for interrelationship/interdependence will be even more obvious as the age structure of society alters with a greater proportion of older and dependent persons, and as medical skills makes it possible for more seriously physically handicapped persons to live more independently and as the current policy of community care for mentally handicapped persons is fully implemented.

The key triangle

As the community becomes the locus of care, and as the delivery of services is increasingly dependent upon cross-professional implementation strategies, there will be increasing opportunities to provide relevant field experience for the professional in training. As indicated earlier, team working does not 'happen' just because legislation requires it. Employers, practitioners and trainers must work together to provide the appropriate interprofessional experience for the trainee professional.

One further aspect of the new legislation is important, that which relates to the arrangements for the funding of training. The training of most of the PAM groups will be controlled at regional level. It is essential that the trainers are in constant dialogue with the regional funders, the professional bodies and the practitioners, the key triangle. Any new practice, informed by research, tested in the field, and funded for training purposes requires the interdisciplinary/interprofessional cooperation of those who make up the key triangle.

The paramedical opportunity is greater than ever before. The remaining challenge is to convince the professional bodies that cooperatively designed joint learning can enhance rather than dilute professional practice. There are encouraging signs that this is now happening. For example, proposals for joint training of physiotherapists and occupational therapists have been well received amongst practitioners, trainers and professional bodies.

Note

1. Complementary medicine has achieved increasing popularity amongst articulate, professional groups, not just because these groups can afford it, but because in emphasizing the 'whole person' it crosses the traditional boundaries of practice of conventional medicine.

References

Department of Health (1990) *Consultative Paper on the NHS Training Framework*. London: Department of Health.

English National Board (1985) *Consultative Document*. London: ENB.

Jaques, D. (1986) *The Report of the Thamesmead Interdisciplinary Project*. Oxford: Educational Methods Unit, Oxford Polytechnic.

Lacey, C. (1977) *The Socialisation of Teachers*. London: Methuen.

National Training Forum (1986) Discussion paper following discussion during 10–11 December 1985 on the education and training of Professions Allied to Medicine. (Limited circulation.)

Physiotherapy (1988) 'Relationship between the physiotherapy and occupational therapy professions'. *Physiotherapy*, **74**(7), July.

Raikes, A.S. and Simpkiss, M.J. (1986) 'Integration of child health services'. *CONCERN* (National Children's Bureau), **61**(5–6), Winter 1986–87.

Interdisciplinarity in the Built Environment

A Post-graduate approach to interdisciplinary studies in the built environment and beyond

John Glasson

Introduction

Interdisciplinarity in the built environment has become a topical issue in recent years. The built environment field is wide, ranging from civil engineering to town planning, although the constituent parts are often packaged together in institutions within a faculty of the name Built Environment, Environment or something similar. The field includes a range of powerful professional bodies, including the Royal Institute of British Architects (RIBA), Royal Institute of Chartered Surveyors (RICS) and Royal Town Planning Institute (RTPI), with extensive membership within the relevant departments in the country's polytechnics and universities.

The various professions are multidisciplinary by nature. For example, 'the art and science of town planning' has an extensive syllabus including design, quantitative methods, social sciences, management, the built and natural environment, information technology and much more. Interdisciplinarity, on the other hand, involves an implication of more jointedness, commonality and overlap between engineers and architects, planners and estate managers and so on. Recent national studies have sought to explore the scope for interdisciplinarity. Of particular note is the CNAA Built Environment Committee's study on 'Interdisciplinarity in the Built Environment' (CNAA, 1991) which involved an examination of potential commonality in professional institute syllabuses, a survey of examples of commonality in higher education in practice, and some tentative proposals for ways forward. Another more broad-brush study was carried out by the National Contractors Group (1989).

But why this interest in interdisciplinarity in the built environment? There are a number of pressures behind it, some more defensible than others. There is a feeling about in some parts of the British construction industry that we are falling behind countries, such as the USA and Japan, in creating the new all-purpose, flexible, innovative and multifunction built environment development manager who is needed to mastermind and bring to fruition the new major projects of the 1990s. This need may be accentuated in the European Community Single Market. Other proponents of interdisciplinarity point to the need for more understanding and appreciation of the respective skills, competences and expertise of one's fellow professionals. Such appreciation does come with practice (which could be argued as continuing education), but some would advocate a greater consideration of such interdisciplinarity within the three, four or five years of professional education. Interdisciplinarity may also help to improve 'team working', and help students to clarify their specific role within the built environment. Others argue on the basis of resources and efficiency; if different subjects are in practice teaching many similar or the same course components, why not have more commonality of teaching, allowing economies of scale in addition to interdisciplinarity?

Issues in interdisciplinarity in the built environment

The maintenance of identity, values and ethos is an important issue in any consideration of interdisciplinarity. It is important both for professional institutes and for academic departments offering professional courses. Such identity, values and ethos can be a source of great strength, leading to high standards and excellence in both education and practice. Any move towards interdisciplinarity must not overly compromise the strengths of such identity. There are important differences in subject areas and unique cores to subjects which must be maintained. Change has an opportunity cost, and the quality of our environment could be the main victim in any ill-considered moves.

Interdisciplinarity also raises issues of scope – how comprehensive can it be? Whilst there may be scope for varying degrees of commonality between civil engineering and building, between architecture and building, between estate management and town planning, for example, there is little scope for commonality across the whole field of the built environment. There are also practical problems of working together – the simple logistical problems of finding enough large rooms and of harmonizing timetables across programmes. With little likelihood of new accommodation quickly, the former is a very serious issue.

The issues already noted have knock-on effects on the issue of the most appropriate academic level of interdisciplinarity. The CNAA Built Environment Committee study considered a range of possibilities, ranging from common foundation years across built environment subjects, to more specialist interdisciplinary projects at the top end of programmes. In the context of the theme of this book, and in the experience of this author, it is strongly suggested that the post-graduate level is a particularly appropriate level for interdisciplinarity in the built environment.

At the post-graduate level, students have the security of a first degree/ professional base and are willing to experiment. It is usually nearer to impending practice and of more immediate relevance. It is also, in the eyes of academic staff, a way of generating large enough numbers to make sometimes vulnerable post-graduate options viable; that is, it enables development. However, on some 'foundation' courses, commonality must be handled carefully. When more than two courses come together, numbers can rise quickly. The specialist training associated with post-graduate courses can be threatened and sub-groups may be necessary if commonality is not to be disabling.

Interdisciplinarity: The case of urban design

A long-standing and well-established interdisciplinary programme at Oxford Polytechnic is the MA/Diploma in Urban Design. This has been jointly offered since 1973 by the School of Architecture and the School of Planning through the Joint Centre for Urban Design. This largely studio-based programme brings together architecture and planning staff, to train students with first degree and/or experience in architecture or planning to operate in the growing field of urban design. The course is one year full-time and two years part-time. It aims to combine students' existing strengths, usually derived both from formal teaching and practice experience, with design training to produce urban designers able to manage the increasingly complex problems of developing urban space and urban form. A major objective is to advance and apply knowledge, skills and abilities in the production of implementable design and management proposals.

The programme is very popular and has an international reputation. At any one time, there are usually 75–100 students on various modes of study on the programme. By its very nature, the MA/Diploma is interdisciplinary and provides a fascinating vehicle for mixing, integrating and developing the research/problem solving/report writing skills of the planner and the design/graphics/presentation skills of the architect. Graduates of the course are in considerable demand from both the public and private sectors in the UK and abroad. The programme is also recognized by the RTPI and RIBA as contributing up to a full one year towards the achievemnt of the professional qualifications of both institutes.

A recent innovation in the course has been its reformulation onto a unit-credit basis. Until recently, because of its 'traditional' studio delivery mode, it was not easily available, in parts, to other post-graduate students in the Environment Faculty at Oxford Polytechnic. The new unit-credit format has opened the course to a much wider field. Thus, for example, students taking the post-graduate planning programmes at Oxford can take a major specialization in urban design. Similarly, the urban design students can take advantage of specialized units in the post-graduate planning programme (e.g. planning law) to extend the planning input of their own programme. Since 1990, the urban design course has also been offered to practitioners, for the purposes of continuing professional development. The unit-credit structure facilitates the offering of parts of the programme as a series of linked short courses, offered in integrated packages, on one day per fortnight, over a period of one term.

Interdisciplinarity and commonality in a wider context

The built environment can be an unrealistic and limiting concept. Several of our new course initiatives involve links with other faculties in the Polytechnic. In 1990, response to new European Community and UK legislation, and to growing environmental awareness, the School of Planning introduced an MSc/Diploma in Environmental Assessment and Management, jointly with the School of Biological and Molecular Sciences in the Faculty of Life Sciences at the Polytechnic. The course brings together a range of natural and social science skills and knowledge, which are needed to assess the impacts on the human and natural environment of major developments, such as motorways, power stations, new settlements and afforestation projects, and to manage those impacts better.

Course development was a fascinating experience, bringing together staff from widely differing backgrounds and with different approaches to experimentation and research. A healthy dose of good humour, an enthusiasm to pioneer course development in this important new field, and the

facilitating device of a common unit-credit system, resulted in a very efficient and effective course design exercise. The resulting course has its pockets
of sectoral expertise, such as prerequisites in Planning and Development,
and in Fundamental Ecology, and a whole range of specialist options (e.g.
pollution control, transport planning), but there is much integrated teaching in the core units in the principles, procedures and methods of environmental assessment and management, and in research methods.

In its first year of operation, the 'take-off' has been remarkable with
approximately 25 students, from a wide range of first degree backgrounds.
There is a shortage of expertise in this new interdisciplinary area and hope-
fully the graduates will have much to offer in this increasingly environ-
mentally sensitive decade, and beyond.

Conclusion

As in most facets of life, progress involves compromise and is most successful
when all the participants can see some benefits. Interdisciplinarity can be,
and can be seen as, a threat. But it does have some benefits and can be vital
in developing the new skills and expertise needed by practice. From experience at Oxford Polytechnic, professional post-graduate education offers
fertile ground for interdisciplinary innovations, and particularly for the
creation of new specializations for the evolving niche markets in the built
environment and beyond.

References

CNAA (1991) *Interdisciplinarity in the Built Environment.* London: CNAA.
National Contractors Group (1989) *Building Towards 2000.* London: NCG.

Collaboration in Course Development – Employers and Educators

Social work

Clare Gillies

Clear advantages of collaboration are often obscured by tension between
employers and educators. This tension is expressed by employers in terms

of the poor quality of students leaving colleges and by educators in terms of the paucity of guidance for new practitioners. These practical worries hide quite deep interprofessional divisions and, as an educator, I am aware of the danger of being seen as one who left a stressful job to become a know-all in a cloistered environment, remote from real work strains.

How then can a group of employers and educators complete a complex task that requires shared responsibility and decision making without being hampered by hidden agenda or power games? One example of our approach concerns the development of a new Diploma in Social Work, which involved Oxford Polytechnic staff and a range of practitioners and employers in local social work services.

The proposal for the new Diploma in Social Work arose following a protracted period of public and professional concern about the quality of social work practice. In autumn 1989 the Central Council for Education and Training in Social Work issued new requirements for the education and training of social workers (CCETSW, 1989). The most significant changes imposed were the ending of the established qualifications of the Certificate in Social Services and the Certificate of Qualification in Social Work and the start of a single award, the Diploma. The new award has to be planned, developed, monitored and managed by academics and practitioners working together as equal partners. The national debate leading to the new proposals was not without acrimony. Teachers on qualifying courses in both universities and polytechnics felt the scapegoat for failings of employers to provide appropriate induction programmes for newly qualified staff and employers. On the other hand, they were pushed by the force of the discussion to make more strident accusations than they might have wished. Collaboration was forced upon these uneasy partners. Moreover, a new programme had to be produced as evidence of the collaborative working and within a limited time. At the beginning of this collaborative exercise we took a good deal of time to identify common aims in educating new practitioners. In this way a sense of commonality and hope was engendered.

The aims were expressed as a determination to:

- attract a wide range of students through the widest possible access and flexible modes of learning
- develop a qualification (DipHE as well as DipSW) which would provide students with a platform for further development and higher qualifications in order to improve quality of service, status of the profession and the self-image of practitioners
- provide a rich quality of educational experience based on the principles of adult learning
- base the course on both polytechnic and work-based learning experience, with the education of employment-based students as well as direct entry students to be fully integrated

- produce competent and reflective practitioners who will become autonomous professionals
- ensure that social work practice was the central educational force.

Agreement of these aims made it natural for the development of a practice curriculum to be the first task and the main focus, thus demonstrating concern of educators, as well as employers, with outcomes, and redistributing the power the educators may seem to have because of their familiarity with curriculum planning and academic notions. Agreed practice outcomes then led to decisions about academic input so that all in the group, whatever their orientation, were willing to contribute as equals in the discussions about what students needed to know in order to be competent in the prescribed ways. We avoided a split between 'perceived do-ers' and 'perceived thinkers' in this way.

The new programme has both practice-based and academic-based modules. Representatives of all the programme providers have planned the curricula for both, thus acknowledging and utlizing the overlap in areas of expert knowledge and skill. In some modules, practitioners are involved in polytechnic teaching and are also the principal assessors. An example of such a module is one directed at examining and challenging the nature of oppression in contemporary Britain. Much of the classroom and academic content draws from sociology, with some from psychology and anthropology; the students are, however, assessed on their ability to use the dynamic of a group to ascertain oppressive practice, their understanding of the nature and impact of oppression and also their competence to challenge and alleviate this by working with groups of people from disadvantaged or minority groups.

It is difficult to devise assessment methods which are rigorous in testing standards of competence achieved and which assess the ability to both select, analyse and apply theory and empirical evidence and to reflect on and evaluate personal practice. Such assessment also requires new ways of approaching the problem as conventional methods tend to give all the power and judgement to the assessor. In this the group have been involved in a newly defined task where all opinions were valued and where both the workplace and the polytechnic seemed appropriate contexts for different parts of the assessment at different stages. Some assignments will be marked by practitioners and by academics and both groups will share responsibility on the boards of examiners.

The experience we have here suggests that inherent difficulties can be managed successfully if due attention is paid to the process of the task and if, in particular, we start from the focus on practice to which all can contribute.

Reference

CCETSW (1989) *Requirements and Regulations for the Diploma in Social Work: Paper 30.* London: CCETSW.

Hotel and Catering Management

Peter Harris

This case emphasizes the collaboration which took place with organizations in the hospitality industry in order to establish an innovatory, industry-linked management development programme leading to the award of a CNAA Master of Science degree in Hotel and Catering Management. The aim of the programme is to give managers the opportunity to integrate their current operational activities with a series of intensive residential weeks of study at Oxford Polytechnic without losing contact with their organizations.

After preliminary discussions had taken place during the autumn of 1986 in the Department of Hotel and Catering Management and at the Polytechnic level, the CNAA was approached to determine whether the proposal was acceptable in principle. The Council's response was positive. Having established that the proposal was educationally sound and operationally manageable in practice, it was considered essential to ascertain the response of industry. However, before this could be effected it was necessary to develop a more detailed outline of the programme in the form of a draft discussion document which could be further developed in consultation with hotel and catering organizations.

After considerable debate the document was produced by a working party and a list containing a broad cross section of hotel and catering organizations was drawn up. In the meantime, Polytechnic approval was sought to constitute a Post-graduate Course Planning Committee (CPC). Approval was given and the CPC assumed responsibility for the proposal in June 1987. The CPC comprised representatives of the department, other Polytechnic departments, an external academic consultant and a senior executive from the hospitality industry.

During the summer of 1987, the chief executives of 17 selected hotel and catering organizations were contacted and subsequently 12 formal presentations and discussion took place over the ensuing months. The organizations approached included hotel companies, the National Health Service, restaurant companies, contract caterers, the civil service catering organizations, public house operators and a major airline.

The aim of the consultations was threefold. Firstly, to demonstrate explicitly the genuine desire to develop a programme in partnership with industry and thereby gain the confidence of organizations. Secondly, to ensure the relevance of course content, assignment work and teaching and learning methods to the personal and professional development of hotel and catering managers. Thirdly, to explore the level of resources the organizations would be prepared to commit to such a programme and also the involvement they would wish to have in its operation.

The discussions were wide ranging and fruitful. Some were concerned about releasing managers from operational responsibilities, whilst others were worried about favouritism. A number of organizations indicated that they were beginning to consider the possibilities of incorporating sponsorship on a Master's course as part of their management development programme. To others the idea was quite a culture shock. However, with the exception of one hotel company, all those consulted gave broad support to the proposal and indicated they would be prepared to recommend the programme within their organizations. None of the organizations was unduly concerned or surprised at the cost of the course. As a direct result of these consultations, the CPC was not only able to develop a state-of-the-art programme in terms of best business practices but in addition evolve a more effective balance between the educational and vocational components.

In the autumn of 1988 a launch event was held at the Polytechnic which 20 organizations were invited to attend, including those who had been consulted. The result was a first intake in January 1989, in which seven of the organizations sponsored managers. In January 1990, eight organizations sponsored managers, four of which had supported managers in the previous year. Furthermore, all the original organizations stated their satisfaction with the programme and conveyed their intention to sponsor managers in the future. For the 1991 entry, 10 organizations were involved, including five which had previously sponsored students.

There seem to be two main reasons for the success of the programme. Firstly, the extensive consultation with the industry ensured that both structure and context were appropriate to senior managers. Secondly, the course team approached the delivery of the course material in a pragmatic way, that is, they developed the sound theoretical framework which underpins the course in ways which addressed the practical concerns and problems of both individual students and the industry as a whole. Consultation and collaboration with employers is thus extremely valuable in developing and delivering a successful and effective course.

Academic Disciplines and Professional Education: The Case of Sociology

Peter George

What is to be taught, by whom, where, and to whom are the teachers to be accountable? These are the key questions about the place of any discipline in education for the professions. The answers vary over time and across professions, but, as noted in Chapter 2, it is possible to identify three stages in the development of education for the professions in which the issues have been addressed rather differently. These can all be illustrated from experience at Oxford Polytechnic.

The first of these stages is the 'apprenticeship' or 'pre-technocratic' stage. At this stage education takes place mainly on the job but some instruction may be given through block, and/or day, release in an associated training school. Sociologists tended to become involved as some professions began to put more emphasis on the social relationship involved in practice. In business and management education, sociologists might be drawn into components of courses, often called 'human relations' or 'behaviourial sciences', which dealt with formal and informal social relationships in work organizations and aspects of the recruitment, selection, training, motivation and welfare of employees. They might also be asked to make a limited contribution to courses concerned with marketing. In other professions the emphasis was more on students recognizing the way in which their clients' social worlds impinged on practice. Culture, community and family and their affect on clients' use of professional services tended to be the focus. Sociologists were not asked to teach sociology, but to cover those bits of the professional syllabus which course leaders assumed were sociological and which they preferred not to teach themselves. More often that not, the time allowed was too little to achieve the restricted goals intended. Some sociologists engaged in such teaching because they thought that it was better done by sociologists than non-sociologists and might lead on to better things. Others refused because it would distract them and could bring the discipline into disrepute. Yet others agreed to undertake the teaching but then taught sociology as they conceived it, rather than what the syllabus demanded – a stratagem which led to disenchantment with 'service' teaching among students and course tutors, for whom the sociologists' contribution appeared to have little relevance. Whatever their response there was little scope for the development of the discipline in professional education at this stage.

In contrast, the second stage, which has been dubbed the 'technocratic' stage in professional education (Schön, 1983, 1987), has given considerable opportunity to develop the role and reality of disciplines such as sociology. Education of professionals tends to take place in schools associated with, or incorporated in, institutions of higher education. Academic disciplines, like sociology, which come to be regarded as providing part of the knowledge base for professional practice, tend to reach the peak of their involvement in education of the professions during this phase. The time allocated to them is often sufficient to introduce students to the basic concepts, perspectives and methods of the discipline, as well as dealing with its application to analysis of issues in the context of the profession and its practice. In a business studies degree, a first year may provide for an introduction to sociology, along with other subjects like economics and law, before turning to the sociology of industry in the second year, and there may also be a choice from a number of more specialized topics like the sociology of industrial relations at a later stage in the course. Similarly, in a social work course, students will be given a basic introduction to the discipline not unlike that offered to an undergraduate student of the discipline, although the topics may be carefully selected and the teaching focused to suit the needs, or the sociologists' perceptions of the needs, of social workers, a selection and concentration which increases as the student proceeds through the course. The sociology curriculum is usually designed and delivered by academic sociologists, perhaps within guidelines supplied by the professions' ruling bodies and after consultation with the professionally qualified tutors who lead the courses. The sociologists who teach on professional courses may themselves be qualified practitioners in some cases, or the subject may be taught by professional tutors who are also qualified and interested in the discipline. This has been the dominant mode of involvement of sociology in professional courses for the last three decades.

In the third 'post-technocratic' stage, increasing emphasis is placed on the acquisition of professional competences. It is not enough to have knowledge; it is necessary to use it effectively in practice to assess people and situations, reach decisions about action, and evaluate the action taken. Each step in this process involves complex judgements, demanding knowledge, intellectual and interpersonal skills and sensitivity to values. The competences involved are seen to be best developed through practice and reflection on practice. Hence understanding the way in which students acquire professional competence through practice and reflection on practice, how skilled practice teachers enable them to do so, and how best to organize the setting for this learning to take place, become the key issues in this stage of professional education. The professional tutor and the practice-teacher are the key figures in the process, apart from the students themselves. The development and delivery of courses depends increasingly on new kinds of partnership between them and academic specialists, and between higher education institutions and employing agencies. In Oxford Polytechnic this new model is emerging in a number of areas like nursing and midwifery, teacher and social worker education.

Each of these phases has a number of implications for the place and reality of academic disciplines. In the first phase, issues include the lack of opportunity for collaborative course development between academic discipline specialists and professional tutors, and external control of the curriculum. In the second phase, there is a range of issues, but one of the key conflicts is over whether the sociologists emphasize the discipline at the expense of its application to professional concerns. This is often associated with disputes over appointments and deployments as, for example, departments responsible for professional courses seek to appoint their own sociologists, and the departments of sociology press for sociologists to be appointed to, or closely associated with them, to make a contribution to mainstream teaching and research in the discipline as well as to its applications.

For academic disciplines the third phase poses particular and new challenges. What is taught must make a manifest contribution to students' developing professional competence; it must be clearly related to practice. If sociology is taught separately from other disciplines, basic concepts, methods and perspectives may be introduced, but through their application to topics which are perceived to be of direct relevance to practice. Indeed, it has been suggested that 'traditional disciplines should be taught in such a way as to make their methods of inquiry visible' (Schön, 1987, p. 322). Increasingly, elements of a sociological approach to phenomena are incorporated in multi- or inter-disciplinary treatment of topics. It demands careful planning and skilful teaching to enable students to think sociologically or exercise the sociological imagination in such a topic-centred curriculum. There is still a demand for sociologists to do such teaching, but often in close cooperation with lecturers in professional studies and practice-teachers. The teaching may take place in college, or the practice setting, but in either case the teaching and learning methods are increasingly those associated with the practicum. For the academic lecturer involved, multiple accountability to students, the teaching team, other academics in the discipline, employing agencies and academic professional validators, is the order of the day.

Experience and developments at Oxford Polytechnic

Sociologists at Oxford Polytechnic have responded in a number of ways to the challenges imposed at these different stages in the evolution of their relationship with professional courses. They have taught in a wide variety of such courses and at different levels, and have been active in course development.

The first phase was already giving way to the second by the time the Polytechnic was designated. Still some sociologists had been persuaded to teach 'human relations' in HNC/HND Business Studies, as well as Institutional Management and Diploma in Management courses, because it was assumed that, as sociologists, they must know about 'human relations'. Some were prepared to effect a compromise between the discipline and the demands of the syllabus; others ignored the 'personnel management' aspects or subjected them to critical analysis in the context of a course based on the sociology of industry. In time the syllabuses were modified and retitled accordingly, and efforts to develop knowledge and competence in the practice of managing people became a separate part of the courses delivered by lecturers in management. Sociologists involved in courses for health visitors, social workers, planners and architects were invited to present the discipline and its approach to such topics as social problems, health, urbanism, family and community studies, and bureaucracy, in as little as four sessions of one to two hours. By demonstrating, but also questioning, the value of what could be done, a case was made for more time for the discipline. Sooner or later this was conceded, but usually only when the courses were lengthened to make room for it and the local course teams gained more responsibility for course design. In this way the scene was set for the transition to the technocratic stage of the discipline's involvement in these courses.

In many institutions the technocratic stage led to the development of substantial departments of sociology providing degrees in the discipline and 'servicing' professional courses. To a lesser extent this happened at Oxford Polytechnic as sociologists associated first with an option in a social studies degree, and then with a field in the undergraduate Modular Course, also taught in community nursing, social work and business studies courses. However, over the last 15 years a different pattern of development has led to the appointment of sociologists in several departments and schools including Social Studies, Planning, Business Studies, Education, Hotel and Catering Management, and Architecture. Those in Social Studies are most closely associated with the academic field in sociology, as well as teaching on professional courses for social workers, nurses, midwives and health visitors. On the other hand, sociologists in the School of Business have been teaching modules in the sociology field in the Modular Course since its inception, as well as on business courses, and modules designed by sociologists in the Schools of Planning and Education for planners and teachers have been adopted as acceptable modules for the sociology field.

Cooperation among sociologists identified with different professional courses and departments has been assisted by efforts to bring them together in a Sociology Subject Committee which has run seminars and conferences, tried to provide a forum for discussion of issues of common concern and those emerging from the whole range of professional courses, and sought to be represented in planning, review and validation of any courses in which sociology or sociologists have a place and in the appointment of staff to fill posts in sociology or held by sociologists. Cooperation has also been encouraged as more professional courses have become part of the Modular Course. While there are advantages for the discipline, as well as the professions, in this pattern of dispersal, it has tended to make it vulnerable, because the academic field is perceived as being sustained by a core team which is too small to make it viable, and because the Sociology Subject Committee, unlike the schools and departments, has no place in the formal structure and can do little to influence school and departmental decisions. Much depends therefore on the ability and determination of the sociologists identified with particular schools to demonstrate the continuing value of sociological research and teaching for the professions with which they are associated.

This has however become more difficult in the last decade as the validity and utility of social research has been called into question by policy-makers and practitioners because it is seen to have failed to contribute much to the solution of either social problems or the development of professional practice. In addition, sociology in particular has often been regarded as a subversive influence in professional education, partly because it is in the nature of the discipline to encourage students to question established social practices and institutions, including those of the professions for which they are pre-paring themselves, and partly because the discipline is seen to be associated with radical critiques of professional interests and power. It is becoming still more difficult as the education of the professions enters the third stage, partly in response to that critique of the professions and their education to which sociologists have indeed made significant contributions.

Full implementation of the third model of education for the professions is still some way off at Oxford Polytechnic, but there is little doubt that it is the model of the future and that there is a secure and influential place for sociology within it. It is leading to new forms of collaboration between sociologists and several professions such as social work, nursing and mid-wifery, occupational therapy, teaching and planning. Increasingly, sociologists are involved, with teachers from the professional schools, and practitioners who coach students in placements, in designing and delivering multi-disciplinary, and to a lesser extent multiprofessional, units of study. There is a two-way traffic, as the professional tutors and teacher-practitioners contribute to the development of sociology in professional courses and sociologists are sometimes drawn into core professional courses. This kind of development may increasingly enable the tacit and explicit theories of practice to engage with the formal theories of sociology, so that researchers and teachers in the discipline and in professional practice can learn from each other (cf. Schön, 1987, p. 321). Recognizing and developing the potential of this form of collaboration for both partners raises interpro-fessional issues which have much in common with those which arise in any other instance of cooperation between professions; issues of culture, identity, status and power, among others.

The growing emphasis on continuing education for the professions, and the development of post-registration and post-graduate courses, open up new opportunities for sociologists. At this level, and among qualified pro-fessionals generally, there is considerable interest in social science research methods, social analysis and forms of critical reflection on practice to which sociological thinking and the sociological imagination can make a signifi-cant contribution. Also at this level there may be more room for sociology because the acquisition of professional competences, which dominates ini-tial training, may require less time.

So the third phase is full of promise for professionally competent and confident sociologists, who are well prepared for inter-professional teamwork, to promote the discipline's contribution to the education and practice of several, if not most, professions.

References

Schön, D.A. (1983) *The Reflective Practitioner.* New York: Basic Books.
Schön, D.A. (1987) *Educating the Reflective Practitioner.* London: Jossey-Bass.

6

The Future: Problems and Prospects

David Watson

The preceding chapters, and the case studies appended to them, give a good indication of one polytechnic's modest but steady progress in meeting a range of challenges connected with the supply of post-experience and professional courses. Two themes, particularly relevant to the Oxford Polytechnic case but potentially generalizable to other institutions, have acted significantly to underpin this process:

1. *Convergence.* The Polytechnic's substantial experience in the design and delivery of unit-based, credit accumulation schemes for mainstream undergraduate education has proved a powerful resource. With this experience, and the administrative infrastructure which accompanies it, it has proved relatively easy to develop an offering which is genuinely agnostic as to mode of study (full-time, part-time, mixed, distance and open). Simultaneously this open, flexible approach to course development has enabled a productive convergence towards offerings which are simultaneously open to students engaged in general, traditional vocational and professional higher education. While there remain significant objections to their cross-fertilization among some of the professional bodies, the case law for its effectiveness and value is now being developed fast.
2. *Management priorities.* In line with the mission statement (quoted in full in Chapter 1) the senior and middle management of the Polytechnic, as well as its various key deliberative groups (such as the Planning, Academic Standards, and Educational Methods Committees of the Academic Board), have made an effective priority of course flexibility and the service of professional needs. Steps taken include:

   - the insistence that all new and revised courses have a regulatory and delivery framework that is potentially agnostic as to mode
   - the dedication of the Polytechnic's well-regarded Staff Release Scheme (allowing teaching and/or support staff release from regular duties in order to develop course material) to PEP projects

- the sponsorship of Polytechnic-wide conferences on relevant issues (such as the implementation of a CATS framework)
- the establishment of a 'fast-track' validation procedure, under the Academic Standards Committee, for approval of distance-learning modes, credit rating of internal and external courses, and 'customized' versions of courses for commercial and industrial partners
- and the support through services of an extended day timetable.

Collectively, of course, these measures have fallen short of the ideal required by those closest to course marketing and delivery. In particular, in common with many other institutions in the PCFC sector, the Polytechnic has proved unable to match the quality of the study environment and its service (including the '*en suite* bathroom factor') enjoyed by the private sector and many universities.

The local priorities for attention and action in developing professional education are thus becoming clearer all the time. This does not, however, reduce in any way the obligation to continue to monitor and anticipate relevant changes in the external environment and their potential impact. Three, in particular, stand out.

The United Kingdom: the 'crisis of professionalism'

Whatever their record in macro-economic terms, and this indeed seems vulnerable to a deep recession at the time of writing, the 1980s – the decade of Thatcherism – were not an unqualified success in terms of training development and professional standards. Despite a bewildering range of initiatives thrown at the problem the full-time staying-on rate in education and training remains stubbornly low for 16–19 year olds, with the resulting structural inhibition on the capacity of higher education to develop and expand. The reluctance of industry and commerce to invest in education and training (with honourable but isolated exceptions) adds to these problems (Cassels, 1990). Some commentators have pointed to a special set of dilemmas for professions and professionals during this period. Not least in the case of the education service itself, the retreat of government commitments to state services has been transferred into an attack on professional values (Marquand *et al.*, 1990, p. 19).

> Professionals are sellers of services who have managed to control the supply of the service they sell. Because they control the supply they can control its market value.
>
> The rhetoric of professionalism is a piece of mumbo-jumbo, designed to conceal this activity from the consumer and to legitimise its consequences. Professional hierarchies, professional disciplines, professional institutions and professional qualifications are the mechanisms through which supply is controlled. Smash the institutions, de-mystify the ethic

and subject the professions to the disciplines of the marketplace, and the sovereign consumer will once again ascend his throne. More important still, the professionals will be forced to abide by the rules of the market and, in doing so, to abandon the corrupting, anti-market values which professionalism engenders and disseminates.

In some ways this is a hard thesis to maintain. As the discussion on inter-professionalism in Chapter 5 indicates most strongly, the 1980s have been an important period of professional consolidation and development. But in another example of convergence, professionals have come increasingly to test their skills and their ability in a competitive market. The resulting value conflicts pose sharp challenges to the 'educational' part of the process of formation of professionals. They also point to the limitations of a definition of professionalism based upon the exclusivity of the traditional professional institutions (medicine, education, law, accounting, etc.) and to a final example of convergence: between the pre- and post-qualification needs of both the traditional professions and the newer fields of so-called 'professional' activity (especially business and management, and the paramedical services). Hence the persistent focus of this volume on post-experience *and* professional education.

Europe: the mutual recognition of qualifications

These concerns also point us towards a wider world. During its imperial past the professional institutions of Great Britain ruled large parts of the world. One only has to review the continuing dependence of many former colonial territories on British law, or to visit the impressive London head-quarters of the major engineering institutions, to achieve a palpable confirmation of this fact. Now we are, as a nation and a society, in danger of being left behind. The new challenges are, geographically, closer to home.

The European Community joint directive on the mutual recognition of qualifications officially took effect in 1991. Its negotiation and implementation has been accompanied by some highly complex manoeuvring by the bodies responsible for professional recognition across the community. Items such as course length, entry requirements, state-specific skills and knowledge, levels of 'practical' training as well as general course content, have all come under intense scrutiny; and progress has been variable. Some professions have taken significant steps, notably the engineering bodies (with the definition of the qualification of European engineer) and the accountants (although there remains a significant difference about the meaning of the term across the various nation states). It is no accident that the chief regulatory framework within which nursing and other paramedical courses have to be developed comes from Europe.

The overall message is, however, clear. Those countries which can offer professional education with a broad range of recognition across the European Community will benefit from the demand for that education. The flow of this demand, moreover, will be facilitated by other decisions of the community centrally, such as the agreement not to discriminate among members of the different states when setting fee levels for individual courses. Simultaneously, there is both direct and indirect evidence of demand from British students for such courses. Included in the latter is the widespread take-up of relevant language study from *ab initio* and intermediate levels, by students whose secondary schooling lacked appropriate provision. In short, they are proving dramatically wrong the prediction of their elders (self-fulfilling in the previous generation's case), that British people lack the interest or the facility to communicate with the Europeans in their own languages.

The challenges to course designers are therefore on several fronts. Making available 'balancing' study such as languages on a wide basis (as is done on the Oxford Polytechnic Modular Course) is one device. Direct negotiation, in partnership with British professional associations, with their European counterparts, towards agreed frameworks for European qualifications is another. Pending the outcome of these, sometime tortuous, discussions in which in several cases (architecture is a prime example) we seem to be marching in the opposite direction from our Community partners, another strategy is to develop joint courses, through formal links with continental institutions, leading to dual or multiple awards, recognized in each of the contributing countries.

The USA: the challenge of reaccreditation

We began this book by reflecting on the national specificity of professional cultures. In Britain, one of the earliest societies to develop an authoritative set of professional institutions, for too long the motion of professional qualification has been of a once-for-all recognition, enabling the licensed practitioner, once the examination or other rites-of-passage (like dinners for intending barristers) have been passed can hang out the shingle and practice until (non-compulsory) retirement. This 'gentlemanly' model fitted the purposes of a stable, hierarchical society, with a high degree of deference and a low premium on innovation.

There is now almost universal acknowledgement that this model of professional formation and professional behaviour has run its course. Societies which are more competitive, internally and externally, have moved to ensure that their professional ranks are more frequently and systematically up-dated, or re-skilled and their professional licences (including indemnification) renewed. The USA leads the way in this process, with many of their professional bodies having mandatory requirements for continuous professional development. What is more, many of the larger national associations (such as the accountants) have developed these 'reaccreditation' programmes outside and in competition with the traditional educational providers.

Some progress has been made in the United Kingdom towards systematic programmes of continuing professional development (CPD) and enhancing the role of professional bodies in continuing recognition. The Law Society and the Royal Institute of British Architects are progressive examples. Other professional bodies have attacked similar anomalies in our professional culture, such as in the Engineering Council, and Engineering Employers Federation's call for tax reform to enable individuals to offset the costs they incur, and the Confederation of British Industry's call for compulsory investment in training (Engineering Council, 1990).

Conclusion

Our goal as educational providers must be to contribute directly and constructively to the solution of these problems and the achievement of these prospects. In this book we have pointed to a number of strategies which appear to have a positive effect: for example, mixed modes of study, an institutional lead in the development of interprofessional courses, and the importance of partnerships with the professional community. However, if there is a unifying theme, it has to be the obligation upon the management of the institution actively to recognize the opportunities provided by, as well as the special needs of, professional courses. Our main argument is about the increasing importance of the institutional dimension; in attracting and distributing resources in an era of constraint; in encouraging the development of appropriate teaching and learning methods; and in 'brokering' the vital set of relationships between sponsors, clients and suppliers.

Beyond the difficulties and rewards of supplying professional education, outlined in this book from a polytechnic perspective, there are some important, ultimately political questions here, about how to reach our goals of becoming a skilled, productive and civilized society. Here, too, the higher education institute has its part to play.

References

Cassels, J. (1990) *Britain's Real Skills Shortage: and what to do about it.* London: Policy Studies Institute.

Engineering Council and Engineering Employers Federation (1990) *Individual Taxation: the need for change.* London: Engineering Council.

Marquand, D. *et al.* (1990) 'Your life in their hands'. *New Statesman and Society,* (27.7.90), 17–24.

Appendix
Professional courses: the Oxford Polytechnic profile (1990–91)

Course title and qualification[1]	Department and Faculty[2]	Subject	Level[3] CATS	Level[3] PRE/CPD	Entry requirements[4]	Type of course[5]	Modes[6]	Length	Numbers (annual intake)	Other information
MA in Education	Education AE	Education	M	CPD	First degree or equivalent Teaching qualification, 3 years' experience	UC	FT PT	1 year FT 2 years PT	3 FT 40 PT	5 specialist tracks
Post-graduate Diploma (PgDip)	Education AE	Education	M	CPD	First degree or equivalent Teaching qualification, 3 years' experience	UC	FT PT	1 year FT 2 years PT	New course target 45 PT	Replacing DPSEs Specialist tracks Joint INSET Scheme with MA
BA (Professional Studies in Education)	Education AE	Education	3	CPD	Teaching qualification, 3 years' experience	UC	FT PT MM	1–2 years FT 2–4 years PT	2 FT 25 PT	Part of Joint INSET scheme with MA and PgDip
Certificate in Professional Studies in Education	Education AE	Education	3	CPD	Teaching qualification, 3 years' experience	UC	FT PT	1 year FT 1 year PT	1–2 FT 100 PT	Part of Joint INSET Scheme
CertEdFE	Education AE	Further education	1	Mostly CPD	Teaching experience	LC	PT	2 years PT	60 PT	Teaching Qualification for further education Partnership with further education colleges to teach course
Certificate in the Education of Hearing Impaired Child (CETHIC)	Education AE	Education of hearing impaired	3	CPD	Teaching experience and qualification	LC	FT	1 year FT	25 FT	Specialized teaching qualification PgDip currently being developed

Appendix (continued)

Course title and qualification[1]	Department and Faculty[2]	Subject	Level[3] CATS	Level[3] PRE/CPD	Entry requirements[4]	Type of course[5]	Modes[6]	Length	Numbers (annual intake)	Other information
Post-graduate Certificate in Education (PGCE)	Education AE	Primary education	3	PRE	First degree	LC	FT PT	1 year FT 2 years PT	120 FT	Gives Qualified Teacher status (QTS)
PGCE	Education AE	Secondary education	3	PRE	First degree	LC	FT	1 year FT	New course target 60 FT	Gives QTS Current subjects: mathematics, modern languages, music
BEd	Education AE	Primary education	3	PRE	2 A levels or equivalent	MC	FT PT MM	4 years FT	100 FT and PT	6 subject specialisms Includes QTS
Diploma in Publishing	Visual Arts, Music and Publishing AE	Publishing	3	PRE CPD	First degree	MC	FT PT	1 year FT	10 FT	
BA/BSc	Visual Arts, Music and Publishing	Publishing	3	PRE	2/3 A levels or equivalent	MC	FT PT MM	3 years FT	50 FT	
Master of Business Administration (MBA)	Business BLHM	Management	M	CPD	First degree or equivalent 2 years' managerial experience	UC	FT PT DL	1 year FT 3 years PT 3 years DL	16 FT 20 PT 52 DL	DL (distance learning) – may be customized
Diploma in Personnel Management (DPM)	Business BLHM	Management	M	CPD	First degree or equivalent Professional experience	LC	PT	2 years PT	30 PT	

Qualification		Subject			Entry requirements		Mode	Duration	Intake	Notes
Diploma in Management Studies (DMS)	Business BLHM	Management	M	CPD	First degree or equivalent Professional experience	LC	PT DL	2 years PT 2 years DL	40 PT 80 DL	DL may be customized
Certificate in Management Studies (CMS)	Business BLHM	Management	?	CPD	BTEC National Cert. or equivalent 3 years' experience	LC	DL	1 year	400	Corporate clients DL may be customized
Certificate/Diploma in Banking	Business BLHM	Banking	1	PRE	GCSE (Certificate) Certificate (Diploma)	LC	FT	1 year FT (each course)	20 (each course)	Overseas banking students
Associate Membership of Institute of Taxation/Association of Tax Technicians	Business BLHM	Taxation	3	CPD	Professional qual. and/or experience	LC	FT PT	1 year FT 1 year PT (Technicians)	20 20	Run alternate years
Institute of Chartered Secretaries and Administrators	Business BLHM	Administration	M	CPD	First degree or Part ACIS	LC	PT	3 years PT	25	Largely public sector Parts 3–4 only
HNC in Business and Finance or Public Administration	Business BLHM	Business, finance, public administration	1	CPD	BTEC National Certificate or equivalent	LC	PT	2 years	40	50/50 Public/private sector
LLB	Business BLHM	Law	3	PRE	3 A levels or equivalent	MC	FT PT MM	3 years FT	25	Gives exemption from common professional examinations
BA/BSc	Business BLHM	Law in combination with another subject	3	PRE	3 A levels or equivalent	MC	FT PT MM	3 years FT	60	Gives exemption from common professional examinations
Diploma (Law Exemption Course)	Business BLHM	Law	3	PRE	First degree in non-law subject	MC	FT	1 year FT	15	Exemption from common professional examination Local non-law graduates

Appendix (continued)

Course title and qualification[1]	Department and Faculty[2]	Subject	Level[3] CATS	Level[3] PRE/CPD	Entry requirements[4]	Type of course[5]	Modes[6]	Length	Numbers (annual intake)	Other information
BA/BSc	Business BLHM	Accounting and finance (in combination with another subject)	3	PRE	3 A levels or equivalent	MC	FT PT MM	3 years FT	70	
BA/BSc	Business BLMH	Business administration and management (in combination with another subject)	3	PRE	3 A Levels or equivalent	MC	FT PT MM	3 years FT	70	
Diploma in Accounting Studies	Business BLMH	Accountancy	1	PRE	2 A levels or equivalent	LC	FT	1 year FT	40	Foundation course
MSc/Post-graduate Diploma	Hotel and Catering Management BLHM	Hotel and catering management	M	CPD	First degree or equivalent and appropriate professional management experience	UC	PT	2 years (MSc) 1 year (Dip)	10	Industry-linked management programme
BSc	Hotel and Catering Management BLHM	Hotel and catering management	3	PRE	2–3 A levels	MC	FT PT MM	4 years FT	90	Includes sandwich programme
BA/BSc	Hotel and Catering Management BLHM	Hotel and catering management (in combination with another subject)	3	PRE	2–3 A levels or equivalent	MC	FT PT MM	3 years FT	30	

Course	Department	Subject	Level	Mode	Entry requirements	UC/LC	FT/PT	Duration	Numbers	Notes
HCIMA Diploma (Hotel, Catering and Instituional Management Association)	Hotel and Catering Management BLHM	Hotel and catering management	2	CPD	HCIMA Certificate/OND/AFL	UC	FT SW	1 year FT 2 years SW	27	Includes industry sponsored students
Diploma in Architecture	Architecture ENV	Architecture	3	PRE/CPD	First degree RIBA Part 2 Exemption	LC	FT	2 years FT	85	
BA in Architectural Studies	Architecture ENV	Architecture	3	PRE	2–3 A levels or equivalent	LC	FT	3 years FT	90	
BSc Estate Management	Estate Management ENV	Estate management	3	PRE	2–3 A levels or equivalent	LC	FT	3 years FT	70	
MA/Diploma in Urban Design (RIBA/RTPI)	Architecture Planning and Urban Design ENV	Urban design	M	PRE/CPD	First degree in Planning, architecture or urban design	UC	FT PT	2 years FT 3–4 years PT	20 FT 20 PT	For recent graduates seeking specialization/entry to profession and practitioners seeking further/professional qualifications. Some common units with post-graduate planning programmes
MSc/Diploma in Urban Planning (RTPI)	Planning ENV	Urban planning	M	PRE/CPD	First degree or equivalent Planning qualifications	UC	FT PT	1–2 years PT 2–3 years PT	10–15 FT 30 PT	For recent graduates and practitioners Some common units with urban design post-graduate programmes
MSc in Housing Studies	Planning ENV	Housing	M	CPD	First degree and housing qualification	UC	FT PT	1 year FT 2 years PT	New	For qualified housing workers seeking professional updating and research skills
Diploma in Housing (IOH)	Planning ENV	Housing	M	PRE/CPD	First degree or equivalent	UC	FT PT	1 year FT 2 years PT	15 10	For recent graduates and practitioners seeking professional qualification

Appendix (continued)

Course title and qualification[1]	Department and Faculty[2]	Subject	Level[3] CATS	Level[3] PRE/CPD	Entry requirements[4]	Type of course[5]	Modes[6]	Length	Numbers (annual intake)	Other information
Diploma in Housing Education	Planning and Education ENV and AE	Housing education	3	CPD	Housing qualification and teaching job	UC	FT PT	1 year FT 2 years PT	New	For housing teachers
MSc in Environmental Assessment and Management	Planning and Biological and Molecular Sciences ENV and LS	Environmental management	M	PRE/CPD	First degree or professional equivalent	UC	FT PT	1 year FT 2 years PT	10–15 FT 15–20 PT	
MA in Historic Preservation	Planning (ENV) and University of Oxford	Building and area preservation	M	PRE/CPD	First degree or professional equivalent	UC	FT PT	1 year FT 2 years PT	New	For built environment professionals, conservation officers, members of conservation groups, etc.
Diploma in Planning	Planning ENV	Planning	3/M	PRE/CPD	Honours degree in planning	UC	FT PT	1 year FT 2 years PT	20	Gives exemption from RTPI examinations
BA	Planning ENV	Planning	3	PRE	2 A levels or equivalent	MC	FT PT MM	3 years FT	65	Combined with Diploma in Planning, gives RTPI examinations exemption
BA/BSc	Planning ENV	Planning (in combination with other subject)	3	PRE	2 A levels or equivalent	MC	FT PT MM	3 years FT	20	
BA	Health Care Studies LS	Nursing and midwifery	3	PRE	2 A levels or equivalent	MC	FT PT MM	4 years FT	125	First entry in September 1990 Specialist nursing areas: general nursing, mental handicap, paediatric nursing, psychiatric nursing

Qualification	Department	Subject	Level		Entry requirements		Mode	Duration	Number	Notes
BA	Health Care Studies LS	Health care studies	3	CPD	Registration in appropriate health care profession	MC	FT PT MM	2 years FT 4 years PT	4 FT 21 PT	For registered health care professionals. Health care studies core, range of clinical and other electives, including teaching qualification. Commenced January 1991
ENB District Nursing Certificate	Health Care Studies LS	District nursing	2	CPD	RGN and post-registration experience	LC	FT	1 year FT	25 FT	Usually seconded Redesigned as part of health care studies degree will include joint teaching/learning with health visiting
ENB Health Visitor Certificate	Health Care Studies LS	Health visiting	2	CPD	RGN and post-registration experience and midwifery/obstetrics qualification	LC	FT	1 year FT	25 FT	Usually seconded Redesigned as part of health care studies degree will include joint teaching/learning with district nursing
ENB Fieldwork/Community Practice Teachers Certificate for Health Visitors/District Nurses	Health Care Studies LS	Practice-based teaching/supervision of HV and DN students	2	CPD	RGN 2 years' experience as health visitor or district nurse	LC	PT	1 year (district nurse) 2 years (health visitor)		Block release and supervised teaching practice. Currently being redesigned as part of health care studies degree
ENB Practice Nurse	Health Care Studies LS	Nursing practice	1	CPD	RGN	LC	PT	30 days	20	Day release
ENB Continuing Education	Health Care Studies LS	Palliative/critical care	2/3	CPD	RGN and experience	MC	FT PT MM			Currently being incorporated into health care studies degree

Appendix (continued)

Course title and qualification[1]	Department and Faculty[2]	Subject	Level[3] CATS	Level[3] PRE/CPD	Entry requirements[4]	Type of course[5]	Modes[6]	Length	Numbers (annual intake)	Other information
BSc	Occupational Therapy LS	Occupational therapy	3	PRE	2 A levels or equivalent	MC	FT PT MM	3 years FT	90	Starts September 1991 following incorporation of Dorset House, School of Occupational Therapy. Replaces former Diploma
Certificate of Qualification in Social Work	Social Studies LS	Social work	2	PRE/CPD	2 A levels or equivalent	LC	FT	2 years	30	Currently being redesigned as two year Diploma, to be located in Modular Course
BEng	Engineering TECH	Mechanical or electronic engineering	3	PRE	2 A levels or equivalent	UC	FT SW	3 years FT 4 years SW	60	
BSc	Engineering TECH	Technology management	3	PRE	2 A levels or equivalent	MC	FT PT MM	3 years FT	New	Starts September 1991 European placement
BA/BSc	Engineering TECH	Microelectronics (in combination with another subject)	3	PRE	2 A levels or equivalent	MC	FT PT MM	3 years FT	20	
BTEC HNC Engineering	Engineering TECH	Mechanical or production engineering	1	CPD	ONC	UC	PT	2 years PT	30	1 day/evening a week release from industry
BTEC HNC Electrical and Electronic Engineering	Engineering TECH	Electrical and electronic engineering	1	CPD	ONC	UC	PT	2 years PT	40	1 day/evening a week release from industry
BTEC HND Engineering	Engineering TECH	Mechanical, electronic, automotive engineering	1	PRE	1 A level or BTEC equivalent	UC	FT SW	2 years FT 3 years SW	30	

HITECC Diploma	Engineering TECH	Mathematics, science, technology	N/A		Non-science A level or age 21 with experience	LC	FT	1 year FT	50	Foundation year for BEng course
BEng (Civil Engineering)	Civil Engineering Building and Cartography (CEBC) TECH	Civil engineering	3	PRE	2 A levels or equivalent	LC	FT	4 years FT	45	Initial professional qualification in civil engineering Thick Sandwich (3rd year)
CIOB Part II (Chartered Institute of Builders)	CEBC TECH	Building	3	CPD	Post-HND	LC	PT	2 years PT	6	Industry clientele – day/evening release
BTEC HND/HNC Civil Engineering	CEBC TECH	Civil engineering	2 (HND) 1 (HNC)	CPD	ONE	LC	FT	3 years FT (HND) 4 years PT (HND) 2 years PT (HNC)	25 HND 20 HNC	PT mode – day/evening release from industry FT mode includes thick sandwich (2nd year)
BTEC HND/HNC Building Studies	CEBC TECH	Building studies	2 (HND) 1 (HNC)	CPD	ONE	LC	FT	3 years FT (HND) 4 years PT (HND) 2 years PT (HNC)	30 FT HND 20 FT HND 30 HNC	PT mode – day/evening release from industry FT mode includes thick sandwich (2nd year)

Key:
1. Where undergraduate degree located in Modular Course, DipHE or CertHE available for students who do not complete course to degree level. Degree usually (Hons) but may be Ordinary if dissertation/synoptic module not taken and passed.
2. Faculties: AE, Arts and Education; BLHM, Business, Languages and Hotel Management; ENV, Environment; LS, Life Sciences; TECH, Technology.
3. CATS level – at exit point. Primarily pre-service (PRE) or continuing professional development (CPD) (some mature, experienced professionals may take the initial/pre-service qualification).
4. Most courses also require GCSE mathematics and English, and may specify particular A level or GCSE subjects or equivalent.
5. Type of course: MC, part of the Polytechnic's (undergraduate) Modular Course; UC, unit/module based on but not in Modular Course; LC, linear course.
6. Modes: FT = full-time; PT = part-time; MM = mixed-mode; DL = distance learning; SW = sandwich.

Notes
1. The audit currently excludes some courses with a strong professional/vocational orientation, e.g. Tourism, Computing Studies (MSc degree and BTEC courses), Diploma in Advanced Study in Anthropology, Diploma in Psychology (BPS recognized) and proposed MSc in Clinical Psychology, Post-graduate Diploma in Petroleum Exploration Geology (see Chapter 1 – discussion of definition, particularly in the light of vocational drift).
2. Current developments include post-graduate programmes in Health Care, Clinical Nursing, Social Sciences, Family Therapy and Architecture.

Index

The Society for Research into Higher Education

The Society for Research into Higher Education exists to stimulate and co-ordinate research into all aspects of higher education. It aims to im-prove the quality of higher education through the encouragement of debate and publication on issues of policy, on the organization and management of higher education institutions, and on the curriculum and teaching methods.

The Society's income is derived from subscriptions, sales of its books and journals, conference fees and grants. It receives no subsidies, and is wholly independent. Its individual members include teachers, researchers, managers and students. Its corporate members are institutions of higher education, research institutes, professional, industrial and governmental bodies. Members are not only from the UK, but from elsewhere in Europe, from America, Canada and Australasia, and it regards its international work as amongst its most important activities.

Under the imprint SRHE & Open University Press, the Society is a specialist publisher of research, having some 30 titles in print. The Editorial Board of the Society's Imprint seeks authoritative research or study in the field. It offers competitive royalties, a highly recognizable format in both hard- and paper-back and the world-wide reputation of the Open University Press.

The Society also publishes *Studies in Higher Education* (three times a year), which is mainly concerned with academic issues, *Higher Education Quarterly* (formerly *Universities Quarterly*), mainly concerned with policy issues, *Abstracts* (three times a year), and *SRHE NEWS* (four times a year).

The Society holds a major annual conference in December, jointly with an institution of higher education. In 1990, the topic was 'Industry and Higher Education', at and with the University of Surrey. Conferences include, in 1991, 'Research and Higher Education in Europe', with the University of Leicester, in 1992, 'Learning to Effect', with Nottingham Polytechnic, and in 1993, 'Governments and the Higher Education Curric-ulum' with the University of Sussex. In addition it holds regular seminars and consultations on topics of current interest.

The Society's committees, study groups and branches are run by members. The groups at present include:
  Teacher Education Study Group
  Continuing Education Group
  Staff Development Group
  Excellence in Teaching & Learning
  Women in Higher Education Group.

Benefits to members

Individual

Individual members receive:

- The *NEWS*, the Society's publications list, conference details and other material included in mailings.
- Reduced rates for *Studies in Higher Education* (£9.75 per year – full price £72) and *Higher Education Quarterly* (£12.35 per year – full price £43).
- A 35 per cent discount on all Open University Press & SRHE publications.
- Free copies of the Proceedings (or Precedings) – commissioned papers on the theme of the Annual Conference.
- Free copies of *Higher Education Abstracts*.
- Reduced rates for conferences.
- Extensive contacts and scope for facilitating initiatives.
- Reduced reciprocal memberships.

Corporate

Corporate members receive:

- All benefits of individual members, plus
- Free copies of *Studies in Higher Education*.
- Unlimited copies of the Society's publications at reduced rates.
- Special rates for its members, e.g. to the Annual Conference.

Subscriptions August 1991– July 1992

Individual members

standard fee	£47
hardship (e.g. unwaged)	£22
students and retired	£14

Corporate members

a) teaching institutions	
under 1000 students	£170
up to 3000 students	£215
over 3000 students	£320
b) non-teaching institutions	up to £325
c) industrial/professional bodies	up to £325

Further information: SRHE, 344–354 Gray's Inn Road, London, WCIX 8BP, UK. Tel: 071 837 7880
Catalogue: SRHE & Open University Press, Celtic Court, 22 Ballmoor, Buckingham MK18 1XW. Tel: (0280) 823388